WHERE DO WE GO *from* HERE?

WHERE DO WE GO *from* HERE?

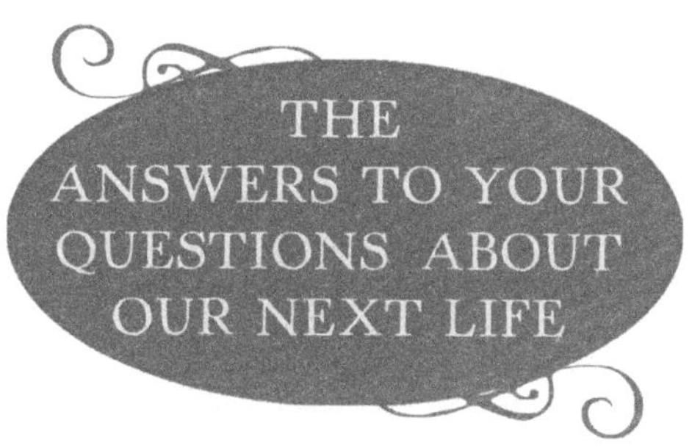

WESLEY M. WHITE
with RACHEL P. ANDERSEN

CFI
An imprint of Cedar Fort, Inc.
Springville, Utah

ISBN 13: 978-1-4621-3768-8

Published by CFI, an imprint of Cedar Fort, Inc.
2373 W. 700 S., Springville, UT 84663
Distributed by Cedar Fort, Inc., www.cedarfort.com

LIBRARY OF CONGRESS CONTROL NUMBER: 2020933728

Cover design by Shawnda T. Craig

Printed in the United States of America

10 9 8 7 6 5 4 3 2 1

Printed on acid-free paper

For all of my adult life, I have been an avid bargain hunter: cars, motorcycles, book, clothes (but not boats; I've never owned a bargain boat). And, when I consider something a bargain, it doubles my enjoyment.

I continued my bargain-hunting ways when seeking a wife. I dated Kay for eighteen months before my mission and two years after, and we have been married for fifty-one years. Every day I marvel and thrill at my bargain. I dedicate this book to her. May our mutual copyright never expire.

CONTENTS

ACKNOWLEDGMENTS

For undertaking this book, I am particularly indebted to two persons. First, my friend Richard McDermott, a successful author and professor, vigorously encouraged me in my efforts and recommended (and in some instances provided) resources that have been immensely helpful. He has proven he is a true friend time and time again.

Second, my son Chad White has been the fastidious and gifted editor this book desperately needed. He examined every word and clarified concepts in each chapter. He wholeheartedly dedicated himself to ameliorating this book, and his impact exceeded my expectations.

Third, Cedar Fort's own Heather Holm has been a delight to work with. I want to be reminded of how great she has been to work with every time I pick up this book.

FOREWORD

Curiosity is a wonderful trait we all share. For example, imagine that you're about to be transferred to work in a mysterious foreign land—how eager you would be to learn all you could about your new assignment. What will the new location be like—the climate, community, population, housing, living conditions, social structure, responsibilities, challenges, transportation modes, neighbors, things to see and do?

You would search the Web, books, anything to get answers. You would seek out knowledgeable people who could answer your queries, guide your planning, and smooth the way for your move.

During your lifetime you may travel to many places, both near and far. Obviously, no matter how much you travel, there will be many places you won't get around to visiting. There is, however, one universal "mysterious foreign land" to which we will all someday transfer—the next life. Of course, it is human nature to oversimplify the unknown, such as our image of angels strumming harps upon eternal clouds. In reality, the spirit world is huge and complex, with at least as much extensive variety as our own planet. In our next existence, we will continue to learn, grow, advance, and progress in preparation to meet our God.

Yet our knowledge of our next life is next to nil. As Robert Ingersoll lamented, "The poor barbarian, weeping above his dead, can answer these questions just as well as the robed priest of the most authentic creed."[1] Through the middle ages and even the Renaissance, if someone had, and then spoke of, a near-death experience, he or she was likely regarded as a witch and burned at the stake. Accordingly, there was a long period when such experiences were kept guarded and rarely told to others. There was also an era when any life-after-death experience was regarded as a religious experience and deemed sacred—not to be shared with others.

Fortunately, we live in a more enlightened era, and the recording of many hundreds of near-death experiences has proven that such experiences happen to both saints and sinners, to people of all races and nationalities, and that they have helped shape people's lives. Numerous "spirit-world guidebooks" have been penned during the past sixty-some years. They've served to open broad gateways of understanding concerning the spirit world—our next stage in our eternal progression. Thousands of people have been granted glimpses of what life after death holds for us. They have died for a short time and then have been sent back to earth life to complete their unfulfilled mortal responsibilities. They have subsequently shared some of the experiences from this preview of our next habitat.

One of the earliest of these spirit-world guidebooks is my book *Life Everlasting: A Definitive Study of Life After Death.* Since it was first published in 1967, it has continued to receive wide-spread acceptance, with more than 500,000 copies sold. It was the forerunner to the landslide of spirit-world guidebooks that soon followed.

In more recent years, many afterlife experiences have been researched and evaluated, gleaning valuable insights that hadn't been emphasized or pointed out with their due clarity. However, they have not been evaluated, correlated, and reinforced by similar accounts.

Wesley White, the author of this book, has proven himself a master of this approach. In doing so, he has formulated new understandings on a significant number of spirit-world situations, locations, timings, descriptions, relationships, and procedures. He's combined newly gathered accounts with neglected details gleaned from experiences recorded in previously published works. These new combinations result in the strengthening and clarifying of a significant number of topics upon which opposing opinions have sometimes been set forth.

In this book, Wes, with my permission and encouragement, has drawn a good number of insights from my book *Life Everlasting*, as well as from numerous other appropriate sources, such as the teachings of General Authorities. As I've reviewed his manuscript, I find he has grasped and magnified a goodly number of new insights from experiences I had cited but which I had failed to adequately explain. Good for him! In his book the scriptural law of witnesses has been put to good use: "At the mouth of two witnesses, or at the mouth of three witnesses, shall the matter be established" (Deuteronomy 19:15).

I have learned new things from this book, and I'm convinced all who read it will also harvest valuable insights. I recommend it to all who seek deeper comprehension of the amazing happenings we will experience when we graduate from mortality and are invited into our merited abode in the next life.

May God bless us all as we do so!

—*Duane S. Crowther*

NOTE

1. Ingersoll, *Greatest Speeches*, 179.

INTRODUCTION

My increased interest in the spirit world began in 1987. It was a rare, beautiful February day in Utah as my wife, Kay, drove along in our old pickup, windows down, a hint of spring in the air. This was long before child seats were required, and our seventh child, two-and-a-half-year-old Russell, stood next to her, his little arm around her shoulders. As she drove, Kay experienced an unanticipated communication from the Spirit. It came in the form of a simple, clear question: "You have had life pretty smooth for a while; are you ready for a trial?" Her mind recoiled with a strident "No!" but her spirit recognized the moment as a time of necessary compliance, and she softly whispered, "Yes."

We were living the dream. We loved being in Utah, and I loved my U.S. Air Force assignment, flying an interesting and fulfilling mission. President Reagan had given the military a substantial pay increase. We moved into a house large enough for our growing family, and Primary Children's Hospital was a wonderful resource for our mentally handicapped fourth child, Debbie. Life was very good. How quickly mortality can take a different turn.

That "turn" came within days of Kay's spiritual communication that she had kept to herself. My aircraft crew was in the office, preparing for a flight, when a crew member announced, "Wes, there's a call for you from your next-door neighbor." That seemed highly unusual. I knew that it had to be something important, whether good or bad. I took the call, and the neighbor blurted, "Russell has been hit by a car!" When I asked if Russell was seriously injured, she hung up.

The drive home was the longest twenty minutes of my life. Did Russell have a broken arm—perhaps a serious head injury? Could it be that he . . . I couldn't bear to let the thought even enter my mind.

I arrived home to the scene of so many ambulances, police cars, and emergency vehicles that I had to park more than a block away. As I sprinted home, a paramedic almost tackled me. He said, "Your little boy did not survive the impact. Do you want to spend a moment with him?"

He pointed me to an ambulance. Little Russell's body was still warm, though disfigured. As I embraced my son for the last time, our stake president approached me and said, "Wes, you are needed in the house. Kay is blaming herself."

Recognizing that severe trials are a part of almost every life, I won't "grieve thee" or "weigh thee down" (Moroni 9:25) with the details of the next weeks, and even years, as we walked "in the valley of the shadow of death" (Psalm 23:4), a valley that is probably familiar territory to you.

Kay and I had each lost one of our parents, but this was different. Our parents had taken care of us, and we were sure that they could take care of themselves in the next life. But Russell was a little child. He had completely depended on us for all of his needs. Was he being cared for now? Did he miss us? Was his spirit an adult or a child? Why was he taken before serving a mission or participating in any of the ordinances of the gospel? What about an eternal helpmeet?

Friends and family would try to comfort us by saying, "Russell was called on a mission to the spirit world." I think you will understand the subsequent whisperings in our minds: *Yes, but he never writes.* We didn't doubt that he lived on, but we very much wanted to know more about his "world." However, that time in our life was too busy for any serious study of the next life. I was enrolled in a master's program, our six other children were struggling with the loss of a sibling, and we were anxiously searching for anything that could enhance our handicapped daughter's life. The spirit world research would have to wait.

The wait was longer than we anticipated, but our callings in The Church of Jesus Christ of Latter-day Saints included experiences that made the reality of the spirit world more evident. These life events—our son's passing, serving in various church callings, sacred personal experiences, and the following quote from the Prophet Joseph Smith—have further inspired this study of the spirit world. Joseph Smith said:

> All men know they must die. And it is important that we should understand the reasons and causes of our exposure to the vicissitudes of life and of death, and the designs and purposes of God in our coming into the world, our sufferings here, and our departure hence. What is the objective of our coming into existence, and then dying and falling away, to be here no more? It is but reasonable to suppose that God would reveal something in reference to the matter, and it is a subject we all ought to study more than any other. We ought to study it day and night, for the world is ignorant in reference to their true condition and relation. If we have any claim on our Heavenly Father for anything, it is for knowledge on this important subject.[1]

Were you to ask, "Isn't there an abundance of books about the spirit world?" I would reply, "Yes, perhaps too many." That's why I have tried to glean the most pertinent and gospel-conforming information available and categorize it according to the questions most frequently asked by members the Church of Jesus Christ. I do so humbly. I recognize that in my weakness I have certainly created an imperfect study. However, in spite of the weakness and any error in this study, I sincerely hope that my research provides some comfort to the grieving and inspires all readers to increase their righteous preparation for the next estate. If not, I have failed.

On the Works Cited page, you will find a short synopsis of the primary sources I have utilized in writing this book, including my brief personal evaluation of the particular source's importance and credibility. For your convenience, I have also included my synopsis of each source in the chapter endnotes when it first appears in this book.

In deference to those who do not read every chapter, there is a small bit of repetition, but only when it is considered important to more than one chapter's theme.

Now, remembering President Dallin H. Oaks' warning that our strengths can become our downfall,[2] trying to abide by President Joseph F. Smith's counsel to avoid "gospel hobbies,[3] recognizing that not all evidence leads to truth, noting that conjecture is dangerous, realizing that some truths are subservient to faith and seem meant to remain so, acceding that I know very little of God and His ways (Isaiah 55: 8–9), reminding myself that my perceptions are merely that, and pledging my best (but imperfect) effort to do so objectively, here we go.

NOTES

1. Crowther, *Life Everlasting*, 17.
2. Oaks, "Apostasy and Restoration."
3. Smith, *Teachings of Joseph F. Smith*, chapter 13.

Chapter 1
PREMORTALITY

Preparing for Judgment Day is like being in a three-act play. Before we entered mortality, we lived with God as His spirit children. We had a pretty good life in that environment, but it was not adequate to prepare us for what we, as children of God, have the potential to become. We required additional experience; we had to be exposed to the "dark side" and to unpleasant experiences and suffering. We had to learn firsthand the difference between good and evil.

Our physical birth began the second act, and it certainly lives up to its billing, providing a very broad range of experience, both joyous and arduous.

The third act is the spiritual existence after we leave this body on earth and move to our next domain, where we will continue, in a quite different venue, to prepare for Judgment Day.

Said Elder Neal A. Maxwell, "If we could see man in continuum [all three "acts"] then we could both understand and rejoice more in the plan of life."[1]

We are currently experiencing act two, and the rest of this book is dedicated to act three. However, here are nine truths about our premortal existence that are essential to our "understand[ing] and rejoic[ing] in the plan of life."[2]

First, we who believe in a premortal existence are a minority. Most Christians believe that only Jesus Christ existed premortally, apparently disregarding God's declaration to Jeremiah, "Before I formed thee in the belly I knew thee; and before thou camest forth out of the womb I sanctified thee, and I ordained thee a prophet unto the nations" (1:5).

Elder Neal A. Maxwell informs us that in Judaism, both the Talmud (the primary source of Jewish religious law) and the Misdrash (a textual interpretation of the Talmud) "clearly teach the doctrine of the premortal existence of souls."[3]

How did Christianity lose such a salient doctrine? Dr. George Ritchie suggests that an anathema against premortal life was passed in the Fifth Ecumenical Council of 533 AD[4]—apparently another casualty of the Great Apostasy. Elder Maxwell suggests that perhaps this doctrine was intentionally deleted in an attempt to decrease our feelings of liability for our behavior in this second estate. In Elder Maxwell's words, "[A knowledge of our premortality] brings much needed identity but also much accountability."[5]

Second, mortality is of much shorter duration than the other two estates.[6] Elder Maxwell taught, "Compared to the first and third estates, the second estate is a mere afternoon.[7]

Third, in the first act we possessed agency, reasoning powers, and intelligence. However, performance there varied greatly. Elder Jörg Klebingat of the Seventy taught:

> Opportunities for growth and learning were widely available. However, equal access to the teachings of a loving heavenly home did not produce a uniform desire among us—Heavenly Father's spirit children—to listen, learn, and obey. Exercising our agency, as we do today, we listened with varying degrees of interest and intent. Some of us eagerly sought to learn and obey. With war in heaven on the horizon, we prepared for graduation from our premortal home. Truth was taught and challenged; testimonies were borne and ridiculed, with each premortal spirit making the choice to either defend or defect from the Father's plan.[8]

Fourth, our performance in that first estate, as well as the characteristics of godhood that we still lack as we transition to mortality, greatly influence our mortal circumstances and assignments. Elder Neal A. Maxwell expressed, "If one's responsibilities [in mortality] are in some ways linked to past performance or to past capabilities, it should not surprise us. If the tutoring one receives bears down especially upon what remains to be refined, why should it be otherwise?"[9] He continues:

> When we say God has a plan, he truly has a plan—not simply a grand scale, but for each of us as individuals, allocating some special talent to this dispensation and some to another. I regard God as the perfect personnel manager, even though he must work with and through all of us who are so imperfect.
>
> I assume, gladly, that in the allocation to America of remarkable leaders like Thomas Jefferson, George Washington, and Abraham Lincoln, the Lord was just as careful. After all, if you've got only one Abraham Lincoln, you'd better put him in that point in history when he's most needed—much as some of us might like to have him now. . . . There cannot be a plan for the whole without a plan for each part." . . . God knew beforehand each of our coefficients for coping and contributing. With regard to our individual traits and personalities, obviously genes and environment play a large part. But more important than we now know is the luggage we bring with us from the pre-mortal world. . . . When in situations of stress we wonder if there is any more in us to give, we can be comforted to know that God, who knows our capacity perfectly, placed us here to succeed. No one was foreordained to fail or to be wicked. When we feel overwhelmed, let us recall the assurance given through Joseph that God, who knows we 'cannot bear all things now,' will not over program us; he will not press upon us more than we can bear.[10]

However, Elder Maxwell wants us to understand that "there are clearly special cases of individuals with special limitations in life, which we cannot now fathom. Like he who was 'blind from birth,' some come to bring glory to God (John 9:1–2). We must be exceedingly careful about imputing either wrong causes or wrong rewards to any of such. They are in the Lord's hands and he loves them perfectly. Some of those who have required much waiting upon in this life may be waited upon in the next world—but for the highest of reasons."[11] It is reasonable to assume that a person who was very valiant in the premortal life might be born into abject poverty because his covenant mortal assignment was among the poorest of the poor.

Fifth, our premortal preparation included both "general education" provided to all mortals, as well as specialized training for our particular mortal mission. Elder Maxwell taught, "There cannot be a grand plan of salvation for all mankind unless there is also a plan for each individual. The salvational sum will reflect all its parts."[12]

Sixth, our first and second estates feature very different learning environments. Said Elder Maxwell:

> Our first estate featured learning of a cognitive type, and it was surely a much longer span than that of our second estate, and the tutoring so much better and more direct.
>
> The second estate, however, is one that emphasizes experiential learning through applying, proving, and testing. We learn cognitively here too, just as a good university examination also teaches even as it tests us. In any event, the books of the first estate are now closed to us, and the present test is, therefore, very real. We have moved, as it were, from first-estate theory to second-estate laboratory. It is here that our Christ-like characteristics are further shaped, and our spiritual skills are thus strengthened. . . . Such a transition in emphasis understandably produces genuine anxiety, for to be 'proved herewith' suggests a stern test, a test that must roll forward to completion or else all that has been invested up to that point would be at risk.[13]

Seventh, as mentioned earlier, our first three estates constitute a continuum. Elder Bruce R. McConkie taught, "All of us are separated by a thin veil only from the friends and fellow laborers with whom we served on the Lord's errand before our eternal spirits took up their abodes in tabernacles of clay."[14]

Said Elder Maxwell, "Individuals have a genetic and an environmental inheritance, each of which is powerfully important. But there is an even earlier bestowal that follows us from our pre-mortal existence wherein our personalities and traits were developed in various ways and in various degrees and strengths. The third bestowal is at least as important as those involving genes and environment. All three combined would, if fully comprehended, give us a true picture of the human personality and how it has been shaped and molded. This would help to explain human differences that are not explainable solely on the basis of genes and environment, varied as these are."[15]

Eighth, we received our mortal mission by covenant. President Dallin H. Oaks said, "Many of us also made covenants with the Father concerning what we would do in mortality. In ways that have not been revealed, our actions in the spirit world influence us in mortality."[16]

Finally, we came joyously to earth. President Ezra Taft Benson taught, "We could hardly wait to demonstrate to our Father and our Brother, the Lord, how much we loved them and how we would be obedient to them in spite of the earthly opposition of the evil one. Nothing is going to startle us more when we pass through the veil to the other side than to realize how well we know Our Father and how familiar His face is to us. If we only knew it, heavenly hosts are pulling for us—friends in heaven that we cannot now remember who yearn for our victory."[17]

This chapter was somewhat of an afterthought. After writing most of this book, I recognized that some knowledge of the first estate would enhance our understanding of the third estate. For me, it has done much more than that. It has improved my understanding of both the evidence and the importance of the Restoration, and the depth and impediment to mankind by the Great Apostasy. It has brought me greater gratitude for the fulness of the gospel to guide and comfort me in the second estate. May this chapter enhance your understanding of the first estate, and may the remainder of this book heighten your understanding of the third estate.

NOTES

1. Maxwell, *The Promise of Discipleship*, 109.
   Elder Maxwell wrote more than thirty books. This one includes a chapter about the spirit world, written just three years before Elder Maxwell's death.
2. Ibid.
3. Maxwell, *But for a Small Moment*, 80. In this book, Elder Maxwell, in his typical elegant prose, compares the emphasis of Joseph Smith's teachings before his incarceration in Liberty Jail with what he emphasized in the years after. Elder Maxwell postulates that the challenges of being the Prophet of the Restoration had kept him so occupied that he'd had little time to deeply study his revelations until he was confined for five months. Two chapters are dedicated to the Prophet's post-imprisonment teachings about premortality.
4. Ritchie, *Return from Tomorrow*, 141.
5. Maxwell, *But for a Small Moment*, 82.
6. Ibid., 88.
7. Maxwell, *The Promise of Discipleship*, 82.
8. Klebingat, "Defending the Faith."
9. Maxwell, *But for a Small Moment*, 99.
10. Ibid., 89–90.
11. Ibid., 99.
12. Ibid., 98.
13. Ibid., 102.
14. McConkie, "God Foreordained His Prophets and People."
15. Ibid.
16. Oaks, "The Great Plan of Happiness."
17. Benson, "Christ—Gifts and Expectations."

Chapter 2
RACHEL'S EXPERIENCE

Rachel is the daughter of one of my best friends who has also been my next-door neighbor for the past three decades. Through this prolonged and close relationship with my friend and neighbor, I naturally became well acquainted with Rachel's personality and high moral character. Having full confidence that it is not in her nature to stretch or unduly hyperbolize, I invited her to put her near-death experience (NDE) in writing so that I could include it within this study. She has graciously participated and provides a firsthand account of an NDE—an experience I have not had. She also provided comments to other chapters. I will introduce those additions by identifying her, as I have done below.

Rachel's Story

I was significantly blessed during my senior year in high school with a trial so great that it became necessary for me to completely rely on the Lord spiritually, physically, and mentally. This trial permanently altered my view of the temporal state of mortal life. Up to this time, I took my physical talents, mind, and abilities for granted and thought I had obtained achievements because of my own work and my own personal determination. Further, I believed I could accomplish any responsibility, challenge, or trial through my well-honed skills.

I had been extremely blessed with a supportive family and enjoyed a close relationship with each of my parents and six sisters. I adored my mom. She was the nearly perfect model of everything I yearned to become: a stalwart, devoted wife and mother. Likewise, my dad was everything I sought in a husband. He was my hero. I appreciated his common-sense advice to "stop and smell the roses" and to "not lean into things so hard." My self-worth and testimony of the Savior had grown day by day, here a little and there a little, with each interaction and obedience to their advice. I felt grateful to spend time as a family, particularly on Sundays and Monday evenings since there was never interruption from television or phone calls during those designated family times. Needless to say, I felt most safe, happy, and loved at home with my family. They were the center of my world—indeed, the biggest influence in my life.

Though not to the same degree, my friends, both at church and school, were also instrumental in my development. I was blessed to be surrounded with good, wholesome peers. I was involved in church and school leadership roles and took each task seriously. I excelled in academics and participated in student government, seminary council, extracurricular clubs, and piano lessons. I served in my Laurel class presidency, Young Women sports, and weekly activities. In short, I had a lot going on. I did my best at all my assignments at all times and aspired to be a good person. I demanded perfection of myself in fulfilling these obligations and was disappointed when I fell short. I honestly believed if I just tried hard enough, worked diligently enough, behaved well enough, and believed in myself, I could steer clear of any future trials or tribulations that would otherwise come.

Naively, I thought of my time on earth as everlasting. I fully identified with the hymn "Because I Have Been Given Much" and acknowledged my responsibility that "I too must give." Although a developing trust in Christ and an increasing testimony of the spirit world were mine, a full reliance and trust in Jesus Christ were yet to be realized.

It was, quite literally, in a split second that my ideal lifestyle was shattered. All my hopes, dreams, and plans for my future seemed to be taken. A drunk driver came out of the dense fog that cold fateful night, ran a red light, and hit my car broadside. I suffered multiple internal injuries and severe head trauma. After several hours in surgery to repair my inner organs, I lay in a deep coma—eyes fixed and dilated, no reaction to pain, and unable to breathe or sustain regular body temperature. My Glasgow coma score was a three, only one point above brain dead. My parents were given no hope of my survival through the next twenty-four hours. My father describes his pain during this time as "bone deep and unrelenting." Yet through a priesthood blessing, Father in Heaven promised that I would not only live but would also have a complete and total recovery. Such a promise was consequent to my past obedience to the commandments and will of the Lord.

After ten long days I opened my eyes. Upon "awakening," amnesia and a long physical recovery followed. It seemed as if all was lost, but over time this has proven otherwise. The mortal miracle was clearly evident, and yet the bigger miracle could not be documented by simple medical facts and data. No one knew of what my spirit experienced. As my physical body lay perfectly still, my spiritual self was elsewhere. The veil that typically separated the mortal and immortal worlds became unusually thin and the spirit world remarkably near. As a result, I personally saw and felt life after mortality. I was significantly blessed to spend time in the spirit world and, furthermore, to recall my sacred visit there.

A soft, delicate white mist of "clean fog" permeated the room-like area in which I found myself. Relief washed over me as I saw before me my paternal grandmother, affectionately known to me as Gram. Although she had died of ovarian cancer six months before, here we stood face to face. Earnest love and tenderness enveloped me. I immediately remembered the eternal friendship we shared with one another. Gram held my gaze, her eyes emitting incredible energy and hope. Never had I known her hair to shine so brightly, her skin to be so smooth and milky white, or her lips and cheeks to be utterly flawless.

While Gram's physical beauty was truly exquisite, it was her extraordinary spiritual beauty that was most captivating. Her goodness and purity radiated a warm light that drew me to her closer. Our visit was intimately private and personal, which emphasized the importance of our time together. The exceptional trust ensured complete understanding. Despite our tenderness, Gram was composed, full of competence, intelligence, and wisdom. Although I was aware of my current dire circumstances, I felt a sure sense of calmness and complete certainty regarding my future. I understood that my decision to continue my temporary earthly existence would affect my eternal existence. That assurance was so profound that all sense of worry or concern was completely alleviated.

Somehow Gram completely understood my thoughts before I could speak. I felt or sensed each answer to my questions. I knew of Gram's gentle encouragement to continue my earthly life. I was silently reminded of promises and blessings not yet fulfilled—most significantly that of motherhood. I realized I could only learn this level of joy and love through experiencing mortality, thereby easily recognizing the extreme importance of life yet to be made possible only through me. I felt no rush in my decision, yet there was no hesitation.

An all-encompassing sureness spread throughout my spirit, and immediately I realized my mortal mission was not yet complete. I knew I must resume my life on earth. I was filled with excitement and a strong sense of purpose. I felt no confusion or fear in my decision. It was as though I had made this choice before, possibly prior to my earthly existence, yet it was necessary to comply once again.

My time in the spirit world was not limited to my personal visit with Gram. I also communicated with my future children, maternal grandfather, and, most important, with the Godhead. I felt of Their presence near and sensed, had I desired, or had it been necessary, I could have visually seen Them, but I somehow knew and accepted that such was not needed. I knew of Father's full attention and support, as if we had spoken face to face. Communication and full comprehension were accomplished through the Holy Ghost. It was as though Father's thoughts were my own. As with Gram, sacred facts and guidance were transferred without voice, resulting in a detailed yet simple, pure perception of God's will. I was determined to be obedient and yet felt assured of His will that I must use my own agency. Such equanimity provided a sense of freedom as the Spirit of Truth testified to my spirit the correctness of my decision.

I returned to school a mere eight weeks following my NDE. I had missed an entire term and was overwhelmed by the amount of work it would take just to be where I was before the accident. A wise and compassionate school counselor determined that "my past was my future," meaning that my previous hard work and good decisions would not go unnoticed. I graduated with high honors, as I had planned. I continued with both speech and occupational therapy through that summer and then moved to Rexburg to pursue my education at Ricks College (now BYU—Idaho) on academic and leadership scholarships. Within two years I graduated with my associate's degree in interpersonal communications. I then transferred to Utah State University, where I earned a bachelor's degree, cum laude, in family and human development.

I have been married for twenty-six years to a wonderful man, Brian, who gained a personal knowledge of Jesus Christ through much fasting and prayer during my recovery. Upon my return to my earthly existence, our relationship seemed natural, as if we had been good friends our entire lives. We experienced the Spirit testify of truth together. As I healed physically—taking my first steps, regaining my memory, relearning to drive, and so on—our connection not only to one another but also to Christ grew. He served a mission in Japan following high school, and upon his return we married a short six weeks later in the Logan Utah Temple. We have four daughters and one son.

Like I was during childhood, today I am most happy at home with my family. I feel so blessed to have achieved my goal and desire of becoming a full-time wife and mother. I feel fulfilled and can think of no greater blessing than that of eternal motherhood. I cherish personal revelation as I am directed in my daily responsibilities, whether conversing with my children, fulfilling my church calling, or researching family history. I also look forward to attending the temple each week, where I feel my love increase for those who are living on the other side of the veil.

I have experienced subsequent trials since my NDE, some of which have again threatened my mortal life. Yet through the power of the Holy Ghost, my spirit can commune with Father in Heaven, and I have realized again and again that He is truly over all. I know life spent in mortality is according to His will. As I plead for aid from those living on the other side of the veil, I am of their awareness and love. I realize pain and sorrow experienced on earth is temporary, but my testimony of the Lord's plan is eternal. A firm belief and absolute trust in an all-knowing eternal Father, as I have experienced in the spirit world, have been necessary to sustain me through such troubling times of uncertainty.

Chapter 3

THROUGH A GLASS, DARKLY

Mankind is by nature curious about our next abode. We ask the following questions: Is there really life after mortality? If so, what will be different? What will be the same? How will we be different, and how will we be the same?

I am extremely grateful for an insight that was given to me years ago. While I was serving as a stake president, a choice sister in the stake passed on. She had been valiant in mortality and faithful through severe health challenges. She was an inspiration to all who knew her. The morning after her passing, I was awakened very early and taught by the Spirit—a sacred experience both rare and precious. The first prompting was, "This is what I want you to teach at Sister ____'s funeral." Interestingly, I had not been asked to speak at her funeral. That request came later the same day.

I was taught that even though I had known this sister for many years, should I be allowed to visit her now, in paradise, I would know her better in just moments than I had during all our many years of mortal association. I was reminded of 1 Corinthians 13:12: "For now we see through a glass, darkly; but then face to face: now I know in part; but then shall I know even also as I am known." In more modern parlance we might say that in mortality, we see other mortals in a distorted view through many "filters." That morning I was taught about four of these mortal filters.

First, in mortality we see every person in his or her fallen state. We see each person's weakness (see Ether 12:27) that comes with this estate. Some of this weakness is general to all mankind (fear, insecurity, carnal desires, pain, pride, illness, and such). But we also have our particular challenges (depression, disability, anxiety, migraine headaches, and myriad more) customized for each of us.[1]

Second, every person we know or see has the adversary nipping at his heels at every turn, particularly taking advantage of our mortal weakness. President Howard W. Hunter taught: "When Jesus had completed the fast of forty days and had communed with God, he was, in this hungry and physically weakened state, left to be tempted of the devil. That, too, was to be part of His preparation. Such a time is always the tempter's moment—when we are weary, vulnerable, and least prepared to resist his insidious temptations. As with Jesus, so with us, relief comes and miracles are enjoyed only after the trial and temptation of our faith."[2] Satan never rests from his efforts to allure us, tempt us, beguile us, and keep us from experiencing joy or strengthening others. And his greatest success comes by kicking us when we are down.

Third, because we know each other only "through a glass, darkly," we often misunderstand others' motives. Perhaps the most well-known example of this is the hunter who returns to his cabin to the cries of his infant son. Seeing his dog's mouth covered with blood, he immediately grabs his ax and kills the dog. It is then that he notices a dead wolf in the cabin and realizes that the dog had protected his infant from the wolf.

A misperception once caused great embarrassment to my wife, Kay. It came early in my career as an Air Force pilot. The Yom Kippur war of 1973 had just begun. My flying squadron put me on high alert and told me to report very early the next morning with personal necessities for ninety days. Just minutes later, I received another call, this time from a man I had previously home taught but who had moved from the area. He said he was back in town and asked to stay with us. I explained that I was about to be deployed and only my wife and three small children would be home. He surprisingly answered, "That's okay," and came over!

When I reported to my squadron early the next morning, they informed us that we were deploying to Israel to assist in the war. Now knowing the destination, I realized I had packed several things I wouldn't need. Another pilot's wife (who didn't have three little kids and company at home) had come to see her husband off. I asked her to take my unnecessary items to Kay.

When she arrived at our home, Kay was busy in the kitchen, and our uninvited guest answered the door. My associate's wife looked at him in disbelief for a moment and then asked for Kay. She gave Kay the things I had sent home and told her coldly, "The plane isn't even off the ground yet."

Now, just for fun, I add an example of a misperception. It seems there was a huge oil well fire in West Texas. The fire departments from several cities were called in, but the heat was so intense that the fire engines could not get close enough to the fire to extinguish it. In desperation, the oil company's regional manager sought help from the fire department of a sleepy near-by town. Shortly, with its siren blaring, a rickety old fire truck arrived on the scene. The fire chief pulled right up to the site of the fire, his crew scrambled off, and from the close proximity they soon had the fire under control. The oil executive was astonished at the bravery of these volunteer fire fighters. He hugged the singed, sooty, still-in-shock fire chief, and expressed that he would donate $6,000 to the small town. The executive then asked the chief how he thought the city would utilize the donation. The chief replied, "Well sir, that's pretty much up to the city council, but I will lobby hard for new brakes for our fire truck."

Fourth, mortality, by design, beats us up. We all bear many scars: emotional, spiritual, mental, or all three. While I was a young missionary serving in Texas, I had pretty well adjusted to having a "24/7" companion, and my companions had somehow learned to endure me. However, one companion seriously challenged my patience. He was a braggart, but he couldn't back it up. He told me repeatedly of his high school athletic prowess: the winning basket, the home run to win the game, the last-second touchdown. However, when the district would gather for preparation day sports, he couldn't deliver. He absolutely lacked the athletic prowess for such stories to be true. How that grated on my nerves! I'm sure my disgust showed in my disposition, but he seemed to respond with even more accounts of spectacular sports "accomplishments."

However, I received a tender mercy. While on exchanges with another missionary, tracting along a dusty Texas road, I aired my frustrations. The other elder listened patiently and then asked, "What do you know about Elder Jones's [not his real name] background?"

The question seemed irrelevant to my frustrations, but I allowed him to continue. He explained that he was from the same small town as Elder Jones, and he began to detail Elder Jones's life, although I must admit that initially I wasn't interested. I learned that Elder Jones was born near the end of World War II while his father was off at war. In fact, Elder Jones's conception happened while his "father" was gone. Elder Jones's mother knew she should write and tell her husband, but she didn't garner the courage until shortly before he returned.

Coming home to a son that he didn't father hit him hard. Elder Jones's "parents" tried to patch things up, but it was tough. Frequent arguments evolved into trying to hurt the other ever more deeply. His mom's infidelity, and the resultant son, became the father's ultimate weapon. He would point to Elder Jones and say to his wife, "Look at what you did to me while I was off to war!"

The family relationship deteriorated to the point that Elder Jones was sent to live with relatives. However, he was no more loved in this new environment than in the old. In some ways, the environment was even worse.

As I listened to Elder Jones's story, and as the elder gave me more details, my picture of Elder Jones completely changed, as did my attitude. He immediately went from "zero to hero." My frustration was gone, replaced by respect—in fact, awe. I marveled that from such a background, he was on a mission. Whenever he impressed me, I marveled that he could do so well coming from his background. When he boasted, I understood. I earnestly tried to make him feel better about himself. To *know* him was to love him.

Though Elder Jones' case may be exceptional, none of us is free from mortality's severe buffetings. To a degree, all of us suffer from some type of posttraumatic stress. The effects show on us, but the causes generally go unknown. What a blessing it was to me to learn about Elder Jones's "scars." As C. S. Lewis expressed in *Mere Christianity*, "Most of man's psychological make-up is probably due to the body; when his body dies all that will fall off of him, and the real central man, the thing that he chose, that made the best or the worst out of this material, will stand naked. All sorts of nice things which we thought our own, but which were really due to a good digestion, will fall off from us: all sorts of nasty things which were due to complexes or bad health will fall off others. We shall then, for the first time, see every one as he really was."[3]

Monsignor Robert Hugh Benson expressed it this way: "All these conditions [the stresses of mortality] bring with them a consequent infirmity of temper. Under the stress of such a life we do not always appear at our best. We can become irritable, or cynical; we think we are possessed of all truth, and inclined to regard as fools others who do not think as we do. We become thoroughly intolerant."[4]

This will be, by far, the longest source synopsis of this book for three reasons. (And because it's so long, I will include it here in the text instead of in the endnotes.) First, Robert Hugh Benson is the author of the three source books that I relied on most heavily. Second, the reason I relied so much on Benson's books is that he is my only source who composed his books as a resident of the spirit world. Therefore, his books provide much more detail about the spirit world than my other sources. Third, this unusual origin of the books begs explanation.

The books were purportedly dictated to Anthony Borgia (his friend in mortality) by Monsignor Robert Hugh Benson, who is dead. Benson (1871–1914) was the son of Edward White Benson, Archbishop of Canterbury. Robert followed in his father's ecclesiastical footsteps and became an Anglican priest. As he studied and began writing—he authored thirty-six books (thirteen of a religious nature) as well as several plays—he became uneasy in his own doctrinal position and converted to Roman Catholicism, becoming a chamberlain to the pope. He accomplished all this before dying at age forty-three. In the spirit world, he recognized the error of the theology he had advocated in mortality and yearned to correct the falsehoods that he, himself, had helped to propagate in the mortal world. Wishing to set things right, he approached those more highly progressed beings who presided over him in the spirit world and requested the opportunity to do so. They told him that he could eventually express his message to the mortal world but not "for some [earth-] years to come." I don't know exactly when he first communicated his message—his effort to "set things right"—but my particular copy of the first of his three books, *Life in the World Unseen*, was published in 1993 by a publishing company named M.A.P. in Midway, Utah. The company no longer exists, and I can find no record of it. My copy of his second book, *More About Life in the World Unseen*, was also published by M.A.P. in 2000. Fortunately, this book provides a rough timeline: It was dictated in 1951 (thirty-seven years after Benson's death). I suppose that *Life in the World Unseen* was dictated years earlier. My copy of Benson's third postmortal book, *Here and Hereafter*, was reprinted in Great Britain by WBC Print (another publishing company for which I have found no record). This third book states that it was first published in 1968.

In spite of the books' unusual origin, Benson's books are three of my major sources. They provide a broader perspective of the spirit world simply because Benson speaks from the grave, with years of spirit world experience (as opposed to a temporary NDE), and he is a skilled communicator.

A dear friend of mine, a PhD and college professor who has written two successful textbooks, has read the three "spirit world" books by Benson as well as several of the books Benson wrote while in mortality. His ardent conclusion, based on the author's writing style, personality, and so on is that all three were unquestionably written by the same person.

These three books are in general harmony with the gospel. I have assiduously attempted to use only material that in no way contradicts the Church's doctrine.

Like the Book of Mormon, Benson's books' profound message is difficult to explain, except for the explanations put forth by the scribe/author himself. Concerning the Book of Mormon, Elder Maxwell counseled us to focus more on its substance than on the process of its production.[5] This may also be a wise approach to Benson's books.

Finally, Monsignor Benson's lives in one the middle realms of the spirit world. Although he visits other realms, most of his information naturally describes his "home" realm.

Now, let's return to Benson's *Here and Hereafter*. When "we leave all the worrying cares of the earth behind us, . . . the beauties and charms of [the spirit world] act like an intellectual tonic; they bring out only that which is and always was the very best in one . . . we are no longer subject to the stresses that produce the unpleasant qualities that were observable in us when we were on the earth. . . . Our tempers were very often sorely tried in those days upon earth. Those times are gone now, and you know us as we really are."[6]

Perhaps Doctrine and Covenants 76:94 references the same principle: "They shall see as they are seen and know as they are known."

And finally, we see others "through a glass, darkly" (1 Corinthians 13:12) not only because of their fallen state, Satan's efforts, and their scars, but also because of our fallen state, Satan's efforts, and our scars. We prejudge others for their national origin, race, color, disposition, age (young or old), religious beliefs, sport team affiliation, physical stature, and hundreds (maybe thousands) more. No wonder the scriptures counsel us to "watch" [perhaps looking for the beam in our own eye] and to "pray always" (Matthew 26:41), as well as warn us to "judge not" (John 7:24), reserving final judgment to Christ Himself.

So here we are: fallen, tempted, misunderstood, and scarred. But a loving Heavenly Father and Jesus Christ, together with the third, unembodied member of the Godhead—the Holy Spirit—unite to provide a way to paradise (even for those who are dead) and a pathway to a celestial eternity for all who merit it. It is their work and their glory, and they have no "distracting hobbies."[7]

And, because of Their divine nature, They maximize mercy and minimize punishment. President J. Reuben Clark said: "I feel that [the Savior] will give that punishment which is the very least that our transgression will justify. I believe that he will bring into his justice all of the infinite love and blessing and mercy and kindness and understanding which he has. . . . And on the other hand, I believe that when it comes to making the rewards for our good conduct, he will give us the maximum that it is possible to give, having in mind the offense which we have committed."[8]

In summation, by suffering the excruciating Atonement, the Savior overcame "the world" (John 16:33) and everything associated with it. Therefore, through our faithfulness and His Atonement in our behalf, we can be completely free of the weakness of mortality, the temptations of Satan, and the scars of mortality.

Although I don't know precisely how the Savior's Atonement applies to those who die and don't attain paradise, we do know that vicarious temple work evidences that the Atonement is still active in their behalf. Although the road may be challenging, "scarlet" sins can "be as white as snow" (Isaiah 1:18).

An Effort to Avoid the Darkness of Human Suffering

I have always enjoyed studying political history, with one caveat: my study, whether of relatively recent events or those in the distant past, cannot be told with any degree of honesty without incorporating the extremes of human suffering that mankind has experienced throughout history. For illustrative purposes, I mention just one form of extreme suffering that mankind has inflicted on other humans—the evil and deliberate torture of prisoners of war (POWs). Having spent a career as a U.S. Air Force pilot, I knew several of the men who were captured during the Vietnam War. During the years that they spent as POWs, they not only suffered deprivation and neglect of every kind, but they were also routinely tortured until the Vietcong were satisfied that they had been sufficiently "broken." Of course, it was not difficult to sense the permanent scars that these men carry with them for the rest of their lives. When I graduated from pilot training, the sober realization that I could possibly be shot down and become a prisoner of war, was never far from my mind. I often heard servicemen speak of the extremes they would go through, or had actually gone through, to avoid this horrible fate.

For example, some years ago, I became friends with a man stationed at the same Air Force Base as I. I was a C-130 pilot (more about that in a later chapter) and he was a B-52 navigator. He passed away a few years ago, so I will not address him by name. However, I will use his title: he was my bishop.

In December of 1972, the Vietnam War was at a stalemate. In an effort to bring the North Vietnamese into serious negotiations, the United States decided to bomb Hanoi and the surrounding area mercilessly, seriously deteriorating its ability to make war. The B-52 was the only bomber capable of this scale of destruction. However, it flew high (giving the enemy additional time to identify it). It was large and therefore not very maneuverable. With all the air defenses in and around Hanoi, the B-52s were essentially sitting ducks.

My bishop was soon deployed to Southeast Asia to fly one of those sitting ducks. A huge bombing run was planned for the night of Christmas Eve. The aircrews realized that many of them would not be coming home. Some would be killed in action. Others would become POWs, and they knew well the torture and deprivation the POWs were suffering. As my bishop's crew considered their predicament, they decided to do whatever was necessary (even if it resulted in death) to avoid becoming POWs on Christmas Eve. As dozens of B-52s lined up for takeoff, laden with heavy bomb loads, my bishop was probably not the only person praying that this mission, on this particular night, would be canceled. But it was not.

As he and his crew approached Hanoi, the ground and sky were lighted with anti-aircraft fire, the rocket launching of surface-to-air (SAM) missiles, and the explosion of bombs. Their aircraft trembled from the shock waves. As they approached their target, they heard and saw what they had most feared: the cockpit light and accompanying siren warning them that an enemy SAM had a radar lock on them. There was little a large, cumbersome aircraft could do once a hypersonic, highly maneuverable SAM was locked onto it.

As the siren wailed and the warning light flashed, the pilot muttered, "Not on Christmas Eve," and put his bomber into a straight-down, full-power dive. The navigator (my bishop) was assigned to keep the pilot apprised of the altitude. He began by calling off each thousand feet— 33,000 feet, 32,000 feet—but the descent became so rapid that he could call out only every three thousand feet: 27,000 feet, 24,000 feet, and so on. As the aircraft approached the ground, the cumulative effect of gravity and engines at full power accelerated far beyond the flight envelope of their plane. Suddenly the plane shuttered violently. The crew cried out, believing they had been hit by the SAM. According to my bishop, the pilot's response was as unbelievable as it was stern: "Calm down! Mach 1!"

Within a few thousand feet of the ground, the pilot tasked the copilot to help him pull the big, overstressed airplane into level flight. With all the strength of both pilots on each one's control yoke, and with the aircraft creaking, groaning, and shuttering, the pilots forced it into level flight.

The hypersonic SAM tried to remain fixed on its target. However, its high speed made for a much larger turn radius, and as it turned to attack its leveled-off target, it plowed into the ground. Bishop told me that the sweetest sound he has ever heard was the sound of silence—when the SAM warning siren ceased.

Flying close to the ground, the crew arrived at their base in Thailand as Christmas morning was dawning. Said my friend, "I of course missed my family, but I have never had a better Christmas."

The B-52 that brought them home was so warped and overstressed that it never again achieved airworthiness. However, the POWs returning from imprisonment in Vietnam brought an interesting and comforting perspective that we will examine in chapter five.

Of course, never having been a POW myself, and having largely escaped the most extreme forms of suffering experienced by mankind throughout the history of the world (such as starvation, severe and incapacitating accidents or debilitating diseases that trap individuals within mortal bodies, and much more), I am ill prepared to truly comprehend or adequately empathize with or comfort those countless individuals less fortunate than I. Rather, I pray that they may take comfort in Jesus Christ and His atoning sacrifice. Only Christ, through His infinite Atonement, possesses perfect and infinite empathy, having "descended below them all" (D&C 122:8). Only He is truly and divinely qualified to succor His people, even erasing the deep, festering scars brought upon mankind by our fallen, mortal state.

Spirit World Basics

Now, as a final prologue, and as a foundation on which we can build, let's look at four basic teachings of Elder Maxwell concerning the spirit world: First, it is vast. He points out that demographers estimate that 60 to 70 billion people have lived on this planet thus far.[9] Second, the "sweat of thy brow" principle will not exist—the chores of this world will not dominate our time as they do in mortality.[10] Third, the spirit world is much more a "house of order" than is mortality.[11] Fourth, the spirit world is part of the second estate: the plan of salvation is still active, and the veil of forgetfulness that prevents us from having a perfect knowledge and understanding of all things is still in place. Although perhaps there may not be atheists in the spirit world, the principle of faith and the requirement to practice that faith through continued learning and progression still apply in the spirit world.[12]

I will add a fifth: every resident of the spirit world arrived there from earth; there is no procreation in the spirit world.

Rachel's Experience

While spending time with Gram in the spirit world, I felt an increase of admiration and respect that I had known for her as a child. The bond we had shared between grandmother and granddaughter remained, yet I was mindful of our eternal friendship. A strong and direct sense of mutual trust and acceptance was evident. I recall our natural and open relationship was greatly enhanced.

Further, my understanding of Gram increased dramatically. Her countenance was completely void of grief and sorrow. In addition, any turmoil of mortality seemed forgotten. The absence of Satan's influence was obvious. I relished in feeling of her true spirit.

The spirit world is a perfect house of order. Indeed, it seemed all things were organized and in proper order. Nothing happened without specific method or conscious decision; exact proficiency was the standard. Further, a comprehensive plan was not only in place but was followed to the very detail by everyone involved in achieving set goals.

NOTES

1. See Maxwell, "Endure It Well."
2. Hunter, "The Temptations of Christ."

3. C. S. Lewis, *Mere Christianity*, 71. The Brethren probably quote the renown Christian theologian C. S. Lewis more than any other Christian who was not a member of The Church of Jesus Christ of Latter-day Saints. Lewis was British and taught at both Cambridge and Oxford. Until age thirty-two, he called himself an atheist, but after being influenced by J.R.R. Tolkien, Rudyard Kipling, and others, he became an ardent advocate of Christianity. He authored more than thirty books (including *The Chronicles of Narnia*), most of them testifying in powerful prose and symbolism of Christ and His attributes.
4. Borgia, *Here and Hereafter*, 123.
5. *A Book of Mormon Treasury*, 5.
6. Borgia, *Here and Hereafter*, 123.
7. Maxwell, "How Choice a Seer!"
8. Quoted in Faust, "The Atonement: Our Greatest Hope."
9. Maxwell, *The Promise of Discipleship*, 105.
10. Ibid., 106.
11. Ibid., 110.
12. Ibid., 111.

Chapter 4
WHERE IS THE SPIRIT WORLD?

Before we jump into the spirit world experiences and expertise garnered from many sources, let's recognize the challenge it is to find words that describe an environment that is totally unfamiliar to us mortals. Benson wrote, "It is I am afraid rather difficult to give a description of some of these things without going beyond the range of earthly minds and experience."[1]

As an example, a challenge the Church faced when translating the Book of Mormon into Polynesian languages was the lack of a word for "snow." Those who have had near death experiences face a similar challenge, attempting to describe an environment in which we have no more frame of reference than Polynesians have of snow. As Dr. Ring concludes from his study of NDEs, "There is absolutely no way in which ordinary human language can communicate the essence of . . . NDEs."[2]

Therefore, as we study what NDErs have experienced and they offer what seems to us peculiar explanations, I may remind you of "the snow principle."

President Brigham Young declared that the spirit world is "incorporated within this celestial system," even "on this earth."[3] Other prophets agree, including President Harold B. Lee: "The spirit world is right here around us."[4]

At least some inhabitants of the spirit world are much more aware of us mortals than we are of them. Brigham Young said, "They can see us, but we cannot see them unless our eyes were opened."[5]

President Young had apparently experienced the difficulty of returning to our fallen world after experiencing a visit to the spirit paradise because he stated, "I have had to exercise a great deal more faith to desire to live than I ever exercised in my whole life to live."[6]

President Joseph Smith taught, "They are not far from us, and know and understand our thoughts, feelings, and emotions, and are often pained therein."[7] Monsignor Benson said, "I did not realize the closeness of the two worlds."[8] I know of no other author who is not a member of The Church of Jesus Christ of Latter-day Saints whose spirit world experiences better parallel the doctrines of the Church. For example, Monsignor Benson says that the spirit world predates this earth, which was in fact patterned after the spirit world.[9] I would suppose that this world, before the Fall, was much like spirit paradise.

Benson also taught of the influence (and of the desire to be of greater influence) the postmortal spirit world has for our mortal world: "The spirit world works constantly to make its power and force and presence felt by the whole earth world, . . . but so little can be done, because the door is usually closed. . . . Think of the evils that could be swept from the face of the earth under the immensely able guidance of wise teachers from the spirit world. . . . Humanity has, in effect, allowed the evil forces to dominate it."[10]

He adds, speaking from spirit world experience, that "your world looks very dark to us, and we try very hard to bring a little light to it."[11]

From that unique perspective, he declared, "Had we withdrawn every element of our influence, the earth would, in a very short time, be reduced to a state of complete and absolute barbarity and chaos."[12]

My great-niece, Camille, recently went through the horror and grief of losing her three-year-old son to an accident. (Coincidentally, both he and I were named after the same Wesley.)

Of this experience Camille wrote:

> In 2018 we were a family of six. We had recently moved from California to Utah. . . . It was Memorial Day and we had big plans to barbeque and roast hot dogs in the back yard and to swim in the community pool. It was 10:15 in the morning and I had just put our third child, three-year-old Wesley, down for a nap. Within an hour I found

myself barefoot in the emergency room of Primary Children's Hospital in Salt Lake City. I hadn't even noticed that I wasn't wearing shoes.

Apparently, when I put Wesley down for a nap, a bolt from his toddler's bed had fallen out. Little Wesley found it, put it in his mouth, and he was choking on it. I expected that it would dislodge easily, but it wouldn't budge. An ambulance and helicopter ride later, my husband, Jeff, and I watched in horror as several nurses frantically performed chest compressions on our little tow-headed boy. His clothes were torn from EMTs attempts at CPR. Soon Jeff and I were looking into the sad eyes of the on-duty pediatric doctor. "I'm so sorry," she began, "your son has experienced an unrecoverable accident." She asked if we were ready to say good-bye. You're never ready to say good-bye. Shock had taken over. We were living one breath at a time, trying to navigate a horrible cloud of shock and grief. Wesley, my sweet enthusiastic little boy, had gone to heaven. . . .

The first few days after Wesley died I felt him extremely close to me. Skeptics may say that it was just wishful thinking or the need to be comforted by something, or the support I felt from friends and family who came running to our aid. While the support of others was overwhelming in a positive way, the hole in my heart was still huge, gaping, wide open and raw. There was no "what if" or wishful thinking, or power on earth that could touch it nor fix it. The times I knew Wesley was nearby were unique, different than any comfort anyone or anything else could provide. I could feel him. Everyone has a spirit. You could even call it a vibe: what you feel when you are around a specific person. It's their presence, a personality, a specific tangible identifiable feeling each person gives off. It's an energy and it's spiritual.

Our loved ones who have passed on are close.[13]

Rachel's Experience

Based on what I perceived during my NDE, I describe the spirit world as being incredibly near. I have witnessed the spirit world's close proximity to the mortal world and realized the separation of the two worlds is transparent. At times, I become overwhelmed with thoughts of how near the spirit world actually is and that of my temporal existence. Firm belief and an absolute trust of an all-knowing Eternal Father confirms the significance of the interdependence between mortal life and the immortal is of utmost importance. Each is fully reliant on the other. The union is perfect, the connection eternal. I am reminded of the reality and feel of the nearness anew as I participate in temple work or attend funerals. At such times, my spirit recognizes the familiarity of heavenly loved ones coexisting on earth, even beside me. I feel of their warm presence in my heart and, quite literally, on my skin. I continue to feel a deep devotion and tenderness toward these many beloved acquaintances. I am conscious of their attachment to me and of their involvement in my daily life.

NOTES

1. Borgia, *Life in the World Unseen*, 29.
2. Ring, *Headed Toward Omega*, 52.
   Heading Toward Omega, like Dr. Moody's books, is a scientific study of NDEs, garnered from 111 people's experiences. Ring focuses much of his book on how an NDE affects the rest of a person's life.
3. Maxwell, *The Promise of Discipleship*, 110.
4. *Teachings of Presidents of the Church—Harold B. Lee*, 58.
5. *Teachings of Presidents of the Church—Brigham Young*, 280.
   Teachings of Presidents of the Church—Brigham Young is a magnificent resource, published by the Church, as a manual for the Melchizedek Priesthood and the Relief Society. Chapters 37 and 38 give great insight into the spirit world. This manual has pronounced credibility because it comes from a prophet, and it has also been through Church correlation.
6. Ibid., 281.
7. Borgia, *Life in the World Unseen*, 6.
8. Smith, *Teachings of the Prophet Joseph Smith*, 326. This book was compiled by Joseph Fielding Smith while he was serving both as an apostle and as Church historian. It is my favorite book of all gospel literature.
9. Borgia, *Here and Hereafter*, 83; Borgia, *More About Life in the World Unseen*, 92.
10. Borgia, *Life in the World Unseen*, 186–88.
11. Ibid., 188.
12. Ibid., 187.
13. Personal correspondence from Camille Packer McConnell.

Chapter 5

HOW MUCH OF MORTALITY IS FOREORDAINED?

Joseph Smith said: "Every man who has a calling to minister to the inhabitants of the world was ordained to that very purpose in the Grand Council of heaven before this world was. I suppose I was ordained to this very office in that Grand Council."[1]

We know that the premortal Jesus Christ volunteered to be the central figure in the Father's plan, He being the only one who could successfully accomplish it. His role was not to eclipse the Father in any way but to glorify Him, in striking contrast to Lucifer's aspirations to "give me thine honor" (Moses 4:1; Elder Maxwell pointed out that Satan said "I" four times and "me" twice in this verse).

The Son then offered, "Thy will be done, and the glory be thine forever" (Moses 4:2). He not only lived up to this by paying the excruciating price of our sins, but also He died for it.

Mosiah L. Hancock recorded his NDE in his journal. He testified that the Savior told him, "'Your time is now come to take your mission on earth,' and he laid His hands on my head, as He had done to others, and set me apart for that important mission. He again said to me, 'I will see you safely thru (sic) until you return again.' I fully believe on that promise."[2] With the personal experience gleaned from her own NDE, author Betty Eadie testified, "I saw that we all volunteered for our positions and stations in the world, and that each of us is receiving more help than we know."[3]

More recently President Nelson's wife, Wendy, gave an address in a worldwide youth devotional where she and the prophet spoke. She implied foreordination:

> So, let me ask you a question: What were you born to do? . . . How I wish you could watch a 10–minute video of your premortal life on YouTube. . . . If you could see yourself courageously responding to attacks on truth and valiantly standing up for Jesus Christ, I believe that every one of you would have the increased power, increased commitment, and eternal perspective to help you overcome any and all of your confusion, doubts, struggles, and problems. All of them! . . . If you could remember who you said you would help while you are here on earth or what anguishing experiences you agreed to go through, that whatever really tough situation you are presently in—or will be in—you would say, "Oh, now I remember. Now I understand. This difficult situation makes sense to me now. With the Lord's help I can do this!" . . . I like to imagine that each of us came to earth with a scroll attached to our spirits entitled ""Things to Do While on Earth." . . My dear friends, pre-mortally you and I were each given wonderful missions to fulfill while here on earth.[4]

My Personal Witness

Allow me to share a couple of personal experiences evidencing that much of our lives were foreordained.

Many years ago, I was called to be a counselor in a stake presidency. For several years I had shaken off promptings of who the president would be and that I would be his counselor. With my wife, Kay, at my side, I received the calling on a Saturday, to be sustained Sunday. I spent much of that Saturday night (and early Sunday morning) in prayer, petitioning confirmation that this call was of the Lord. The heavens were silent. The following morning, at the moment I was released as a high counselor, the answer came: I had been called to precisely what I should be doing at the time. I was also given a spiritual addendum. My subsequent callings would be stake president and then mission president.

The year after my release as stake president, I was called to preside over a Spanish-speaking mission, with the particular mission assignment still undecided. We later received a tentative call to serve in Argentina while the Brethren further evaluated our family situation. They decided that our handicapped daughter would best be served stateside, and we were called to the Florida Orlando Mission. I am ashamed to say that we were crushed. We wanted to serve in Latin America! We wanted to be immersed in Spanish. We were deeply disappointed, though we tried to pretend, and to project, that we were pleased. The mission presidents' seminar was like salt in the wound. It seemed as though every president and wife read our tags and said, "Florida Orlando, that's where we hoped to serve."

However, the disappointment that had haunted us for seven months was completely eradicated within days of arriving in Orlando. "Our" missionaries were serving there! It was tangible! We weren't totally immersed in Spanish as we had anticipated, but we were totally immersed in the spiritual confirmation that these were the missionaries with whom we were foreordained to serve. We had to, and were blessed to, serve where they were; our call was divinely orchestrated, as was theirs.

At that time, missionaries from the United States or Canada who were serving in overseas missions and had returned home for any reason were reassigned to a mission in one of these two countries. Because of the diversity of people living in the Florida Orlando Mission, our missionaries were called to serve in one of four different languages. Therefore, many missionaries who were reassigned from overseas and spoke one of those languages were assigned to serve with us. The Lord soon confirmed that there are no surprises to Him. We learned to promise these reassigned missionaries that if they would "thrust in [their] sickle with [their] might" (D&C 4:4) they would teach at least someone they were foreordained to teach. Almost all reassigned missionaries took this to heart and saw the promise fulfilled. One such missionary taught and baptized an older and childless widow. After his mission, she flew from Florida to Utah so that he could serve as her husband's proxy for their sealing. (And she also bequeathed the elder a substantial portion of her estate when she passed away.)

One of our daughters had this truth reinforced while serving her mission. She was delighted with her call to serve in the Spain Barcelona Mission. However, after she had served there for nine months, we received a call from the Missionary Department. Because of a visa problem, she would be reassigned to a stateside mission. We worried for her; she loved serving in Spain so much. However, the Lord granted her three tender mercies.

First, when she arrived in the Texas McAllen Mission, her president allowed her to call home. We learned that rather than being emotionally crushed, she was very much at peace. She explained that when she was initially told of the change, she was devastated. But when she said her prayers at the end of the day, the Spirit communicated to her that this was exactly as it should be. She had served the first half of her mission in her own behalf, but the second half she was to be a proxy for her younger brother who had died in childhood. Like many of our Orlando missionaries, while in her reassigned stateside mission, she found that "foreordained" family. After her mission, we were privileged to meet that special family.

Second, my mission as a youth encompassed her mission, and her mission president permitted her to attend the dedication of a meetinghouse in a small Texas town where I had served forty years earlier.

Third, when she fell in love, she learned that her fiancé had served in that same mission. They discovered that there were people whom they both knew and areas where both had served.

Betty Eadie taught, "There are far fewer accidents here than we imagine, especially in things that affect us eternally. The hand of God, and the path we chose before we came here, guide many of our decisions and even many seemingly random experiences we have. It's fruitless to try to identify them all, but they do happen, and for a purpose. Even experiences such as divorce, sudden unemployment, or being a victim may ultimately give us knowledge and contribute to our spiritual development. Although these experiences are painful, they can help us grow. . . . Under the guidance of the Savior I learned that it was important for me to accept all experience as potentially good."[5]

Character from Crisis

I was an Air Force officer in 1973 when the American prisoners of war returned from Vietnam. It was one of the most touching and impactful events of my life. Some of our men had been held as long as seven and a half years. All had been incarcerated with inadequate clothing, food, and medical care. They were brutally tortured, some to death. Most remained true to our country under horrendous circumstances, and they still carry the lifetime physical and emotional scars.

After their releases, they were, of course, not ready to immediately integrate into their military professions. As part of their healing process, many Air Force ex-POWs were sent on extensive lecture tours to Air Force bases around the world. I was privileged to hear many of them speak. The POW experience influenced them very differently. Some declared that they now knew there is no God. Others stated just as vehemently that now they knew that there is a God. However, every ex-POW declared that though he would never want to endure such an experience again, he was glad that it had happened to him. Each said that he had learned things from that horrible experience that he treasured.

In my mind, their expression is a microcosm of our mortal lives. I believe that when we have died and have passed through the veil, we will remember many trials of mortality that we would never care to suffer again. But, at the same time we will be very grateful for each experience. We will then recognize it as essential to our eternal welfare and character.

The entire universe is in harmony, each of us experiencing our tailor-made trials that define, and qualify us for, our role in the universe. Dr. Neal said of her NDE, "I began to visualize a reasonable analogy for our individual lives: each of us is like a small piece of thread that contributes to the weaving of a very large and very beautiful tapestry. We, as single threads, spend our lives worrying about our thread—what color it is and how long it is—even being upset if it becomes torn or frayed. The complete tapestry is far too large for us to see and of too complex a pattern for us to appreciate the importance of a single thread. Regardless, without our individual contribution, the tapestry would be incomplete and broken."[6]

A friend and neighbor of mine experienced an NDE. He concludes his book with the following:

> God has created a perfect plan for your life. Just like how each fingerprint is different, and each snowflake is different and unique, your life was designed by God and your highest self to create the perfect path for your learning. This is how much God values you. He spent the time to create a perfect path with perfect teachers to come into your life so you can learn what we need to grow. You are a perfect snowflake crystal and there is a perfect path for you to follow to find your highest self. Imagine the beauty of each unique snowflake and then imagine the beauty of all of the snowflakes combined that make up a blanket of whiteness that covers the earth. God loved you enough to create an individual plan for your growth and happiness. I testify how much He loves you, and how unique and special you are to Him. I pray that you will begin to see yourself as God sees you.[7]

Dr. Moody's research indicates that "NDEers come back with a sense that everything in the universe is connected."[8] Moody has not personally experienced an NDE, but he has made a study of the experiences of others and has written several books.

Moody tells of a no-nonsense businessman who said, "One big thing I learned when I died was that we are all part of one big, living universe. If we think we can hurt another person or another living thing without hurting ourselves, we are sadly mistaken. I look at a forest or a flower or a bird now, and say, 'That is me, part of me.'"[9]

Many other NDEers have marveled at the great order in the spirit world, as well as the universe. Dr. George Ritchie expressed it this way: "He has created an extremely orderly universe which operates as result of definite laws and principles."[10]

The Lord's declaration that "my house is a house of order" (D&C 132:18) perhaps refers to our homes at the first level, the temple at a level, the paradisiacal earth at another, paradise at still another, and ultimately the universe.

Our "Tailor Made" Trials

Brigham Young implied that our particular trials are customized: "Every trial and experience you have passed through is necessary for your salvation."[11]

Said President Hinckley, "In the heroic effort of the handcart pioneers, we learn a great truth. All must pass through a 'refiner's fire,' and the insignificant and unimportant in our lives can melt away like dross and make our faith bright, intact, and strong. There seems to be a full measure of anguish, sorrow, and often heartache for everyone, including those who earnestly seek to do right and be faithful. Yet this is part of the purging to become acquainted with God."[12]

Elder David S. Baxter succinctly taught that "our character is shaped in the crucible of affliction."[13] President Harold B. Lee echoed Baxter's sentiments when he said:

> Some of us have been tried and tested until our very heart strings would seem to break. I have heard of people dying with a broken heart, and I thought that was just a sort of a poetic expression, but I have learned that it could be very real experience. I came near to that thing, but when I began to think of my own troubles, I thought of what the apostle Paul said of the Master, "Though he were a son, yet learned he obedience by the things which he suffered; And being made perfect, he became the author of eternal salvation unto all those who obey

> him" (Hebrews 5:8, 9). Don't be afraid of the testing and trials of life. Sometimes when you are going through the most severe tests, you will be nearer to God than you have any idea, for like the experience of the Master himself in the temptation on the mount, in the Garden of Gethsemane, and on the cross at Calvary, the scriptures record, "And behold, angels came and ministered unto him" (Matthew 4:11). Sometimes that may happen to you in the midst of your trials.[14]

Note how closely these statements parallel Sister Eadie's declaration earlier in this chapter.

Some years ago, a member of our stake was driving to Salt Lake City. She sang in the Tabernacle Choir at Temple Square, and she was traveling to participate in their weekly program. Her automobile hit a patch of ice. She lost control and also lost her life, leaving her husband with six children, ages eighteen months to thirteen years. When I met with her husband a few months later, the Spirit testified to me that we, as mortals, cannot even begin to understand how eternally important it is that this brother remained true to his covenants under such a trying circumstance. Like the POWs who were grateful for the experience, I believe that this faithful brother will be postmortally grateful for the experience and that he will be crowned with glory for being true and faithful as he diligently keeps his covenants.

In conclusion, we turn to President Hinckley's perspective on life in his eighty-third year: "I have experienced my share of disappointments, of failures, of difficulties. But on balance, life has been very good."[15]

Rachel's Experience

I believe I not only agreed but was also willing and eager to participate in my NDE before coming to earth. As time passes, I become more certain of this. For I would not, could not, have the life I have been blessed with presently if not for my NDE. Most obvious is my choice of an eternal companion. It was through much fasting and prayer that Brian received a lifetime testimony of Christ and of His gospel. Upon our continued faith and obedience, the highest of blessings of eternal family is now obtainable. This evidence proves to me that I knew and approved of my great challenge prior to earthly life.

In addition to promises given me in my patriarchal blessing, many other coincidences further convince me I agreed to the many trials prior to my mortal life. A few examples include:

- *Paramedics were across the street of the accident and had learned earlier that day how to treat head injuries.*
- *The hospital of choice specialized in traumatic head injuries but was unable to send a life-flight helicopter due to the dense fog. Instead I was flown to another hospital, which proved to be of more importance to my recovery because of their renown rehabilitation program.*
- *The fog cleared precisely over the intersection, allowing the helicopter to land.*
- *The best surgeons in the world were on-call that night.*

President Joseph F. Smith observed how "we often catch a spark from the awakened memories of the immortal soul, which lights up our whole being as with the glory of our former home. Thus, when we say, 'I know,' that realization is rediscovery; we are actually saying 'I know—again! We agreed to come here and to undergo certain experiences under certain conditions."[16]

NOTES

1. Smith, *Teachings of the Prophet Joseph Smith*, 365.
2. Crowther, *Life Everlasting*, 98.
   Life Everlasting: A Definitive Study of Life After Death, by Duane S. Crowther, was first published in 1967. More than 150 pages were added thirty years later. Crowther was the "pioneer" member of the Church to write thoroughly researched books concerning the future of this world and of our hereafter. *Life Everlasting* addresses not only the spirit world but also man's journey all the way to (hopefully) exaltation. The book received immediate widespread readership due to the quality of writing and the many new concepts it introduced, supported by meticulously researched documentation. More than 100,000 copies were in circulation by 1970, when other books began to be published on the subject and received worldwide circulation. Many of them cited it and referred to the experiences Crowther cited. Over the years, sales of *Life Everlasting* have climbed to more than a half-million copies, and the book retains its position as one of the most significant books on life after death in print. As one of the most renowned "restored Church of Jesus Christ" authors of all time, Crowther has written fifty-six books, nearly thirty on gospel topics.
3. Eadie, *Embraced by the Light*, 53. Number one *New York Times* best seller. Sister Eadie was raised on an Indian reservation. She converted to The Church of Jesus Christ of Latter-day Saints but drifted into inactivity, until after her NDE. The book's sales demonstrate its appeal. It is an easy, joyful read centered on divine love. It has inspired multitudes and provided hope to the heavy-hearted.

4. Worldwide Youth Devotional, President Russell M. Nelson and wife, Wendy Watson Nelson. "Hope of Israel," June 3, 2018. Broadcast from the Conference Center.
5. Eadie, 68–69; see also Romans 8:28: "And we know that all things work together for good to them that love God."
6. Neal, *To Heaven and Back,* 102. Also a number one *New York Times* best seller. The Christian author is by profession an orthopedic surgeon. While her book adds but little new information about the spirit world, it is a powerful testate to the love of God.
7. Rampton, *You Were Born a Warrior*, last paragraph.
8. Moody, *The Light Beyond,* 42. Offers synopses of the work of several researchers. Moody believes that NDEs have two irrefutable proofs: (1) everyone he knows of who has experienced an NDE (including those researched by others) has returned happier and more dedicated to higher purposes than before, and (2) many who have experienced an NDE can give precise detail of the events in the hospital (even some that occurred in a different area in the hospital) while the person was "dead." For example, Moody cites the experience of a woman, blind from age eighteen, who had an NDE at age seventy. She could precisely describe events, persons, and even medical instruments utilized while she was "dead."
9. Ibid.
10. Ritchie, *Return from Tomorrow*, 14. Essentially "opened the door" for lending credence to NDEs. It has been immensely popular. My copy, printed in 2004, was from the thirty-third printing. A friend gave it to me when our son was killed, and I subsequently passed it on to a friend who lost his wife in a traffic accident. It provided both comfort and insight, and I suppose that pattern has happened thousands of times. Dr. Ritchie is not a member of the Church, but he speaks positively about it.
11. Young, *Discourses of Brigham Young*, 345.
12. Hinckley, "Faith in Every Footstep."
13. Baxter, "Faith, Fortitude, Fulfillment."
14. Lee, Area Conference, Munich, Germany, 1973.
15. Hinckley, "Lessons I Learned as a Boy."
16. Quoted by Maxwell, "Premortality, a Glorious Reality."

Chapter 6

ARE OUR DAYS NUMBERED?

Oh, this thing we call death! It may take us within an instant of leaving the premortal life or wait until our years of mortality have extended into triple digits. Anna, an elderly temple worker mentioned in the New Testament, is a scriptural example of the latter. She was one of the first to recognize the infant Jesus Christ as the long-anticipated Messiah. Luke informs us that her husband had lived only seven years into their marriage and that she had been widowed for eighty-four years (see Luke 2:36–7).

Some who are full of life are taken in a moment. Others yearn for death but linger for years or even decades. Is life's duration random or foreordained?

Let's begin by examining what three of our prophets have taught. While Joseph Smith was suffering in Liberty Jail, the Lord promised him, "Thy days are known, and thy years shall not be numbered less (D&C 122:9).

Elder Richard G. Scott stated in general conference, "We will live for our appointed life span."[1]

Ecclesiastes 3:2 states, "[There is] a time to be born, and a time to die."

In the booklet "Tragedy or Destiny?" President Spencer W. Kimball taught, "I am confident that there is a time to die, but I believe that many people die before 'their time' because they are careless, abuse their bodies, take unnecessary chances, or expose themselves to hazards, accidents, and sickness."[2]

Author Lee Nelson tells of a woman about to die who expressed that her deceased husband still loved her and wanted her to come with him. "When is he coming for you?" someone asked. She replied, "In the morning, early." She died the next day at 6:15 a.m.[3]

Regarding when mortality begins, Betty Eadie, an NDEr and convert raised on an Indian reservation, stated, "I learned that spirits can choose to enter their mother's body at any stage of her pregnancy. Once there, they immediately begin experiencing mortality."[4]

Referring to children who die young, she said, "I understood that their death had been appointed before their births—as were ours. These spirits did not need the development that would result from longer lives in mortality."[5] (For more information concerning infant mortality, see chapter 16.)

Eadie also taught about violent death: "If our deaths are traumatic, the spirit quickly leaves the body, sometimes even before death occurs."[6]

I am particularly grateful for this last statement because several years ago I was asked to speak at the funeral of a dear friend's granddaughter who had died in a fiery crash. I was prompted to say that her spirit left her body an instant before the accident. I had never heard such doctrine, so I was comforted when I read Eadie's words and felt that I was probably responding to a valid prompting.

From the much pondering I have done since our young son died many years ago, I believe that a child who has not reached the age of accountability will not die unless he or she is foreordained to do so. These little children cannot be tempted by Satan (see D&C 29:47), and they are not accountable for placing themselves in danger or even capable of recognizing many hazardous situations. Our God is a God of justice, and it would not be fair to take a child's life when he puts himself in peril and is not accountable for doing so—unless he was foreordained to a brief mortality.

Modern-day prophets offer two reasons for children to be taken at a young age. The Prophet Joseph Smith said, "In my leisure moments [there were probably not many of those!] I have meditated upon the subject, and asked the question, why is it that infants, innocent children, are taken away from us, especially those that seem to be the most intelligent and interesting. . . . The Lord takes many away even in infancy, that they may escape the envy of man, and the sorrows and evils of this present world; they were too pure, too lovely, to live on earth; therefore, if rightly considered, instead of mourning we have reason to rejoice as they are delivered from evil, and we shall soon have them again."[7]

Second, President John Taylor called them noble spirits who could not be spared from important spirit world assignments for an extended time, so they were "furloughed" to a short mortal experience before resuming greater works.[8]

Further, the non-foreordained early death of a child would be unfair in mortality as well as in eternity. On one side, the child would miss choice opportunities to learn by the experiences of mortality, and on the other, he would gain the celestial kingdom whether or not he or she merited it. To the question, "are [children] automatically saved?" Elder Bruce R. McConkie replied, "To this question the answer is a thunderous yes, which echoes and re-echoes from one end of heaven to the other. Jesus taught it to His disciples. Mormon said it over and over again. Many of the prophets have spoken about it, and it is implicit in the whole plan of salvation."[9]

Elder McConkie added: "We may rest assured that all things are controlled and governed by Him whose spirit children we are. He knows the end from the beginning [D&C 130:7], and he provides for each of us the testing and trials which He knows we need. President Joseph Fielding Smith [Elder McConkie's father-in-law] once told me that we must assume that the Lord knows and arranges beforehand who shall be taken in infancy and who will remain on earth to undergo whatever tests are needed in their cases."[10]

It is probably not possible for us to understand every aspect of the complex celestial equation of death, but we can, with certainty, say that there are no unanticipated arrivals into the spirit world.

I personally have not experienced the type of near-death experience related in this book. However, I have had a very-near-to-death experience that is as vivid in my memory as it was the day it happened.

I was a U. S. Air Force pilot, flying a four-engine cargo aircraft designated as a C-130. It's a big machine: 100 feet long, 150-foot wingspan, 100,000 pounds net weight, 175,000 maximum takeoff weight. It is extremely versatile with many configurations: hurricane hunter, gunship, search and rescue aircraft, test bed for experimental flight, launch and control aircraft for remotely piloted vehicles, and more. I still have great love for it and great respect for its capabilities. It has taken this former Idaho farm boy to much of the world and allowed him to participate in the test and evaluation of new technology. I loved flying it. I preferred a day of flying to a day off. However, for an unforgettable moment, one of those days of flying appeared to be my last.

The C-130 was a natural choice when the U. S. Army asked the Air Force to test the feasibility of adding a smaller tank to its inventory, one that could be airdropped wherever needed. However, this "small" tank would still weigh 36,000 pounds. I was one of the pilots on the crew that was tasked to test the feasibility of airdropping something that large. We flew to Edwards Air Force Base in the Mojave Desert, where much of the Air Force's test and evaluation takes place. We loaded our "bird" with a special crate manufactured to the proposed tank's approximate size and filled to the tank's approximate weight. It was an unusual load: old cement, scrap iron, lead, and other heavy junk boxed together in a huge container. This loaded crate was placed very precisely into our C-130: a few feet too far forward or aft would take the aircraft's center of gravity out of safe parameters. A nylon strap was attached to the crate. The other end of the strap was attached to three 100-foot diameter parachutes (together, larger than a football field) which were stowed in the back of the aircraft. The plan was to fly over the drop zone where the loadmasters in the back of the plane would release the parachutes into the airstream, pulling the load from the aircraft. Those same three chutes would then slow the load as it descended to the ground. At least that was the plan.

And for a moment it worked. The chutes deployed, the aircraft shuddered and slowed substantially from the added drag, and the load began sliding toward the back of the large aircraft. The test engineers would soon have the data they needed. HOWEVER, as the load was located at the very aft of the C-130, the strap between the load and the chutes broke!

We have all been on the high end of a teeter totter when the person at the bottom gets off. This was about the same. With the center of gravity at the very aft of the aircraft, if began to fall out of the sky, the tail down, and the nose straight up. Everything was happening so fast that I didn't have the time to think of the long-term result: my wife a widow with six children. I recalled that if someone is killed at Edwards Air Force Base while flight testing, a street on the base is named for him or her. The strange thought came to me, "I will get a street named for me, but when someone asks how I died, expecting an answer such as 'he was attempting hypersonic flight' or 'he had engine failure but rode his plane into the ground to avoid hitting a school' the answer would be "he backed his airplane into the ground.'"

As we fell backward, I looked at the cockpit instrument that the Air Force calls a vertical velocity indicator. It indicated that our descent rate was 4,000 feet per minute. Knowing that we were three thousand feet above the ground, I quickly did the math: we had 45 seconds to live!

I'm alive to tell this story, so obviously something "good" happened. With our four engines at full power, and with the C-130's huge flight control (called the elevator) creating lots of drag, gravity overcame the friction holding the load in the aircraft, and it fell out onto the dessert floor. I generally dislike negative g-forces, but the negative "g"s from our aircraft swapping ends felt wonderful! I have computed that at that point we were 12.5 seconds from crashing.

We were relieved, but we still had a huge problem. An airplane requires airflow over the wings for it to fly. Our airspeed was "zero," and we were just a few hundred feet above the ground: the ordeal was not yet over. We lowered the nose and skimmed the dessert floor until we gained enough airspeed to fly. We probably clipped the tops off a few cacti and frightened some jack rabbits, but we were alive!

We flew around the base perimeter until we gained some composure, and then we landed at the base. The test team members on the ground were there when we taxied in, and they looked like the proverbial deer in the headlights. I was the first crewmember to exit the aircraft, and I immediately said, "I want to talk to the flight test engineer" (the person who would have computed the necessary tensile strength required for the strap that broke). No one would identify him, which was probably a good thing: like Nephi of old, I am large in stature and the end result would have most surely been unfavorable for both of us.

I am grateful for the allotted years since then. Many of my greatest experiences have occurred after that nearly fateful day.

However, had this whole ordeal ended tragically, you would still have the money you spent for this book in your pocket, and any angels who may have been watching over me that day wouldn't have been as exhausted.

Rachel's Experience

My NDE has taught me of the temporary nature of earthly life. An ever-loving and all-knowing Father ultimately determines how long we spend in mortality. I have acquired a deep trust that my earthly existence is according to His will. I trust Father in Heaven has a plan for me, including the length of my mortal life. I promised in the spirit world to be obedient to His plan. Therefore I need not fear.

NOTES

1. Scott, "How to Obtain Revelation and Inspiration for Your Personal Life."
2. Kimball, "Tragedy or Destiny?" 9.
3. Nelson, *Beyond the Veil,* 141. Lee Nelson is a popular author and a member of the Church. Volume 1 of *Beyond the Veil* is a compilation of near-death experiences primarily from members of the Church. There is little commentary.
4. Eadie, *Embraced by the Light,* 95.
5. Ibid., 95–96.
6. Ibid., 83).
7. Smith, *Teachings of the Prophet Joseph Smith,* 196–97.
8. Hill, *Angel Children,* 55. This book was given to us by a friend soon after the death of our son. It had given her some comfort after her personal loss of a child. Written by a woman who had lost a child, it quotes Church leaders, scriptures, and several prominent members of the Church . It supports the concept that the death of a child is not haphazard but rather foreordained.
9. *Doctrine and Covenants Student Manual,* 355.
10. Ibid., 356.

Chapter 7

TEMPLES IN THE SPIRIT WORLD

The word *temple* has different meanings among different peoples. We call some edifices in the ruins of Central and South America temples. The ancient Greeks had the Temple of Hephaestus in Athens. Borobudur is a large Indonesian Buddhist temple. Angkor Wat in Cambodia is the largest Hindu temple. So, when considering whether temples play a role in the spirit world, the short answer would be that it depends on how you define a temple. To help us differentiate, I will note which sources in this chapter are members of The Church of Jesus Christ of Latter-day Saints by using the label "LDS." Those who are not members of the Church are not specifically noted.

Heber Hales (LDS), speaking of his vision of the spirit world, said he beheld "a wonderfully beautiful Temple [sic], capped with golden domes."[1]

Wilford Woodruff (LDS), while serving as President of the Church, spoke of seeing Joseph Smith in the spirit world: "In the night vision I saw him at the door of the temple in heaven."[2]

Rebecca Springer wrote, "Upon the summit . . . a Temple (sic) stood, whose vast dome, massive pillars and solid walls were of unsullied pearl, and through whose great mullioned windows shone a white radiance that swallowed up the golden glow of the twilight and made it its own."[3]

Monsignor Benson provides more specifics. As a new arrival in the spirit world, he detailed a visit to one of the cities there. He said, "Here were fine broad thoroughfares of emerald green lawns in perfect cultivation, radiating like the spokes of a wheel, from a central building which, as we could see was the hub of the whole city. There was a great shaft of pure light descending upon the dome of this building, and we felt instinctively—without Edwin [the guide] having to tell us—that in this temple we could gather to send up our thanks to the Great Source of all, and that there we should find none other than the Glory of God in Truth."[4] He also remarked on the ineffable beauty of the flowers on the temple grounds.[5]

From this same "tour," he explained that inside these temples "we spirit people are conscious of the eternal thanks that we owe to the Great Father for giving us such unbounded happiness in a land of which so many upon earth deny the reality."[6]

Benson also detailed a meeting in a grand temple: "We could hear the sound of music, but whence it came I knew not, because there was no sign of any musicians. The music was evidently provided by a large orchestra—of strings only, for there were no sounds of the other instruments of orchestra."[7]

Benson spoke of attending a beautiful concert, incomparable to any in this mortal world:

> The sanctuary, which was of spacious dimensions, was filled with many beings from higher realms, with the exception of a space in the center, which I guessed was reserved for our visitant. We were all of us seated, and we conversed quietly amongst ourselves. Presently we were aware of the presence of a stately figure of a man with jet-black hair, who was closely followed—very much to my surprise—by the kindly Egyptian that we had met at Edwin's house on the boundary of our realm. To those who had already witnessed such visitations, their arrival was at once the indication of the coming of the high personage, and we all accordingly rose to our feet. Then, before our eyes, there appeared first a light, which might almost be described as dazzling, but as we concentrated our gaze upon it we immediately became attuned to it, and we felt no sensation of spiritual discomfort. . . . It was toned down to accord with ourselves and our realm, . . . and in the center there slowly took shape the form of our visitant. As it gained in density we could see that he was a man whose appearance was that of youth—spiritual youth—but we knew that he carried with him to an unimaginable degree the three comprehensive and all-sufficing attributes of Wisdom, Knowledge and Purity. . . . His movements were majestic and

> as he raised his arms he sent forth a blessing upon us all. We remained standing and silent while our thoughts ascended to Him Who sent such a glorious being. . . . It is not possible for me to convey to you one fraction of the exaltation of the spirit that I felt while in his presence, though distant, of this heavenly guest. But I do know that not for long could I have remained in that temple while he was there without undergoing the almost crushing consciousness that I was low, very, very low upon the scale of spiritual evolution and progression. And yet I knew that he was sending out to me, as to us all, thoughts of encouragement, of good hope, of kindness in the very highest degree, that made me feel that I must never, never despair of attaining to the highest spiritual realm, and that there was good and useful work ready for me to do in the service of man, and that in the doing thereof I would have the whole of the spiritual realm behind me—as they are behind every single soul who works in the service of man.[8]

The above quote mentions the Egyptian. Monsignor Benson refers to him several times, offering insights into his appearance and even his personality. He does the same with one he calls the Chaldean. Both abide in higher realms and interact several times with Benson and his associates. Benson mentions that both have spent thousands of earth-years in the spirit world and that when both are present, the Chaldean presides. The thought has entered my mind that the Chaldean could perhaps be Abraham and the Egyptian Joseph of old, but this is purely speculation.

It appears to me that temples in the next life probably vary somewhat in their functions from realm to realm. In Benson's realm, his temple experience seems to almost parallel a general conference of the Church on earth. But the vision seen by President Woodruff, with Joseph Smith at the door of the temple, suggests a temple in spirit paradise.

It seems that a common purpose of all temples is to (1) provide a special place in which to worship and express thanks to God, (2) feel of His great love for all of His children, and (3) understand the opportunity and receive encouragement to progress toward becoming as He is.

Rachel's Experience

Understandably, many fear the transition of mortal to immortal existence. It is human nature to feel anxious about the unknown. Based on my NDE, I am comforted by the memory of life beyond the grave. I feel tremendously blessed to have discovered the unconditional love of my deceased ancestors and enjoy knowing of their nearness. I rely on their support greatly, particularly in times of tribulation or uncertainty. I find much relief as I call upon them for direction and reassurance in doing the Lord's will.

When my earthly time is complete and it is time to enter the spirit world, which is the next phase of the Lord's plan, I know I will not fear. Although my mortal mind no longer recalls the intricacy of the next life nor understands the vastness of eternity, I know my spirit did. I may feel uncertain up until the precise time of transition, yet I have faith I will remember and comprehend with exactness the details of eternal life, as I have before. I will at last be able to see the faces of my beloved heavenly friends and relatives, and any fear will be replaced with complete peace.

NOTES

1. Crowther, *Life Everlasting*, 164.
2. Ibid., 234.
3. Springer, *My Dream of Heaven*, 100. This book was recently published, although the experience related therein occurred shortly after the American Civil War (1861–65). I include this book because the author, not a member of the Church, references eternal marriage as a part of her NDE.
4. Borgia, *Life in the World Unseen*, 43.
5. Ibid., 99.
6. Ibid., 51.
7. Ibid., 99–100
8. Ibid.

Chapter 8

ARE GUARDIAN ANGELS REAL?

Opinions about guardian angels vary. Elder Bruce R. McConkie states in *Mormon Doctrine*: "There is an old and false sectarian tradition to the effect that all men—or if not that, at least the righteous—have guardian angels, heavenly beings of some sort who attend them and exercise some sort of preserving and guarding care. It is true that there are many specific instances in which angels, by special assignment, have performed particular works whereby faithful people have been guarded and preserved. But to suppose that either all men or all righteous men have heavenly beings acting as guardians for them runs counter to the basic revealed facts relative to the manner in which the Lord exercises his watchfulness over his mortal children."[1]

Other Church leaders have offered a different take. Joseph Smith referred to his guardian angel just two weeks before his martyrdom. He recounted a recent dream in which he said, "I was riding out in my carriage, and my guardian angel was along with me."[2]

Hyrum Smith told Edward Hunter, who had recently lost a child, "Your son will act as an angel to you; not your guardian angel, but an auxiliary angel, to assist you in extreme trials."[3]

Parley P. Pratt, in *Key to the Science of Theology*, stated that while mortal bodies sleep, "their kindred spirits, their guardian angels hover about them with the fondest affection, the most anxious solicitude."[4]

In the April 1989 general conference, President Ezra Taft Benson declared, "I promise you, dear children, that angels will minister unto you also. You may not see them, but they will be there to help you, and you will feel their presence."[5]

In the October 1998 general conference, President Dallin H. Oaks remarked, "Most angelic communications are felt or heard rather than seen."[6]

President James E. Faust taught, "There are invisible hosts watching over us even as they did Elisha of old. I believe that unseen hosts tend us as we seek to do the will of the Lord."[7]

With just over a year to live, President Faust taught:

> We do not consciously realize the extent to which ministering angels affect our lives. President Joseph F Smith said, 'In like manner our fathers and mothers, brothers, sisters and friends who have passed away from this earth, having been faithful, and worthy to enjoy these rights and privileges, may have a mission given them to visit their relatives and friends upon the earth again, bringing from the divine Presence messages of love, of warning, or reproof and instruction, to those whom they have learned to love in the flesh.' Many of us feel that we have had this experience. Their ministry has been and is an important part of the gospel.[8]

More recently, Elder Jeffrey R. Holland, in the Church's general conference of October 2008, presented a talk entitled "The Ministry of Angels." After speaking of Adam and Eve's expulsion from the Garden of Eden, he proclaimed, "But God knew the challenge they would face, and He certainly knew how lonely and troubled they would sometimes feel. So He watched over his mortal family constantly, heard their prayers always, and sent prophets (and later apostles) to teach, counsel, and guide them. But in times of special need, He sent angels, divine messengers, to bless His children, reassure them that heaven was always very close and that His help was always very near."[9]

Holland presented several examples from the scriptures of visitations of angels and then said: "From the beginning down through the dispensations, God has used angels as His emissaries in conveying love and concern for His children."[10]

Holland continued, "Usually such beings are *not* seen. But seen or unseen they are *always* near. Sometimes their assignments are very grand and have significance for the whole world. Sometimes the messages are more private. Occasionally the angelic purpose is to warn. But most often it is to comfort, to provide some form of merciful attention, guidance in difficult times."[11]

Near the end of his discourse, Holland testified, "My beloved brothers and sisters, I testify that . . . always there are those angels who come and go all around us, seen and unseen, known and unknown, mortal and immortal."[12]

A year later, Elder Robert D. Hales, after explaining his recent time of great suffering and pain, said:

> As I studied the scriptures during this critical period of my life, the veil was thin and answers were given to me as they were recorded in lives of others who had gone through even more severe trials. . . . I also learned that I would not be left alone to meet these trials and tribulations but that guardian angels would attend me. There were some that were near angels in the form of doctors, nurses, and most of all my sweet companion, Mary. And on occasion, when the Lord so desired, I was to be comforted with visitations of heavenly hosts that brought comfort and eternal reassurances in my time of need.[13]

Others who have studied the spirit world or who have experienced an NDE also testify of guardian angels. Monsignor Benson proclaimed, "Every soul that has ever been, and is to be, born upon the earth-plane has allocated to him—or her—a spirit guide."[14]

To those who do not believe in these constant guides, he warned, "That day will be whereon they meet in the spirit world their own guide, who probably knows more about their lives than they do themselves."[15]

Betty Eadie, in her bestselling book, expressed what most of us believe: "Each of us is receiving more help than we know."[16]

Our Personal Experience

Kay and I had almost identical experiences after our toddler was killed in an auto-pedestrian accident. Hers came just after she had picked up his broken body from the street and was rocking it, before emergency personnel arrived. Mine came just after we returned home from the funeral.

In each case, we sensed keenly that the house was full of rejoicing spirits. The joy they emitted was greater than we had ever felt—a celebration beyond anything we had ever known—but our pain and grief at the time was so great that we were angry with them for reveling so joyously while our suffering was so great. However, over time, as the wounds from our loss have partially healed, we are comforted that our little two-year-old who had depended so greatly on us was elatedly received by others whom we suppose were deceased family members.

Angels Ministering within the Spirit World

Now let's examine the angels who minister in the spirit world. Assignments there (besides those previously mentioned) include preparing clothing for those about to enter that realm or guiding newcomers (this is often performed by a family member or former friend).[17]

These minister angels also serve as messengers to earth, as well as perform missionary work, teach the gospel, and construct buildings in the spirit world.[18] The "housing boom" there, of course, never ceases and is much accelerated in times of war and pestilence.

Just as the temples in mortality have recorders, recording is a significant assignment in the spirit world. The scriptures refer often to what we call the Book of Life (there are twenty-three scriptural references to it in the Topical Guide). Many who have visited the spirit world speak of recorders who are assigned to keep accurate records of a person's life and who then add those records to the Book of Life.[19]

A temple patron told me that his eyes were opened while doing baptisms for the dead and he saw a spiritual recorder both writing down the names and stating them. The recorder pronounced some of the names quite differently than they were pronounced in the ordinance. If this is the case, what a comfort it is to us when we struggle with proxy name pronunciation in the temple.

Spirit World "Halls of Rest"

The last ministering angel assignment I address in this chapter requires some background. Before this study, I supposed that everything that mortal life does to "beat you up" remained in the grave, all by the power of the Atonement. I have learned that "there are some burdens so great that we even carry them over with us into the spirit world."[20] Some afflictions have been so great, so prolonged, or so tragically sudden that they impact not only the body but also the mind, and there they remain after death as an impediment to progress.

Benson explained, "The earth world, in its blind ignorance, hurls hundreds of thousands of souls into this our land, but those who dwell in the higher realms are fully aware long before it happens, . . . and a fiat goes forth to the realms nearer the earth to prepare for what is to come. These dire calamities of the earth-plane necessitate the building of more and more halls of rest."[21]

Benson continued, "In the great halls of rest there are expert nurses and doctors ready to treat those whose last earthly illness has been long and painful, or whose passing into spirit has been sudden or violent. . . . These homes are a standing monument of shame to the earth world. The percentage is low, deplorably low, of people who come into the spirit world with any knowledge at all of their new life and of the spirit world in general. All the countless souls without this knowledge have to be taken care of."[22]

Monsignor Benson spoke of visiting two halls. The first was occupied by the spirits of those who had suffered lingering illness before dying. "Immediately after their [death] they are sent gently into a deep sleep. In some cases the sleep follows instantly—or practically without break—upon the physical death. Long illness prior to passing into the spirit world has a debilitating effect upon the mind, which in turn has its influence upon the spirit body. The latter is not serious, but the mind requires absolute rest of varying duration. Each case is treated individually, and eventually responds perfectly to the treatment."[23]

The most difficult part of ministering to these souls is when they awaken. "It has to be explained to the newly awakened soul that he has 'died' and is alive. . . . When the true state of affairs has been gently and quietly explained them, they often have an urgent desire to go back to earth, perhaps to those who are sorrowing, perhaps to those for whose care and welfare they were responsible. They are told that nothing can be done by their going back, and that others of experience will take care of those circumstances that are so distressing them."[24]

Benson also visited a larger hall where those whose passing had been sudden and violent receive special care. These also were immediately placed into the state of a resting mind. When they awake, "the suddenness of their departure added far greater confusion to the mind. . . . The passing over had been so sudden that there seemed to them to be no break in their lives. Such people are taken in hand quickly by bands of souls who devote all their time and the whole of their energies to such work." Benson lauds "these gentle, patient helpers wrestling mentally—and sometimes almost physically—with people who are wholly ignorant of the fact that they are 'dead.'"[25]

He also noted that the ruler of the realm and visitors from higher realms make frequent visits to these halls.

Not surprisingly, Monsignor Benson, after the completion of his orientation, requested to serve in the halls of rest. He tells us that he subsequently received that assignment.

Rachel

There were many times during my recovery that were very upsetting, frustrating, and discouraging. Looking back, I am amazed at the degree of pain and fear I endured. I attribute this miraculous ability not as my own but to the Savior and His remarkable power to provide mercy and grace. I truly lived without physical distress, mental anguish, or emotional sorrow during this time. I had the "privilege of soaring among immortal beings and of enjoying to a certain extent, the presence of God."[26]

I was constantly aware of countless immortal beings, of past and future generations, and knew of their love and tenderness they had for me. Gram was not my only guardian angel but rather one of many who spiritually and physically supported and protected me throughout this great trial. This blessing continued for several weeks, if not months. These unseen angels still bring much needed peace to my spirit even today. I feel of their concern daily. Though the veil is no longer transparent to me, and despite the difficulty of seeing my guardian angels physically, I know of their presence and feel of their love.

NOTES

1. McConkie, *Mormon Doctrine*, 341.
2. Crowther, *Life Everlasting*, 262.
3. Ibid.
4. Ibid., 120–22.
5. Benson, "To the Children of the Church."
6. Oaks, "The Aaronic Priesthood and the Sacrament."
7. Faust, "The Voice of the Spirit."
8. Faust, "A Royal Priesthood."
9. Holland, "The Ministry of Angels."
10. Ibid.

11. Ibid.
12. Ibid.
13. Hales, "The Covenant of Baptism."
14. Borgia, *Life in the World Unseen,* 183.
15. Ibid., 185.
16. Eadie, *Embraced by the Light,* 53.
17. Top, *Glimpses Beyond Death's Door*, 156–57. Brother Top has served in significant positions in the Church Educational System and as a stake president and mission president. The book provides insights from leaders of the Church and from persons who have experienced NDEs. Brother Top is mentioned in note 1 to President Oaks' talk "Trusting in the Lord" in the October 2019 general conference (churchofjesus-christ.org/study/ensign/2019/11/17oaks?lang=eng).
18. Crowther, 191.
19. Crowther, 310.
20. Borgia, 73.
21. Ibid., 115.
22. Ibid., 167–68.
23. Ibid., 36.
24. Ibid., 37.
25. Ibid., 38.
26. Smith, *Journal of Discourses,* vol. 19, 260.

Chapter 9

DIVISIONS IN THE SPIRIT WORLD

Most Christian religions teach that in the afterlife, every postmortal being is assigned eternally to heaven or hell. In contrast, members of The Church of Jesus Christ of Latter-day Saints understand that there is no such thing as an eternal hell. The Church views hell as a temporary abode: "Nevertheless, it is not written that there shall be no end to this torment, but it is written endless torment. . . . For, behold, the mystery of godliness, how great it is! For, behold, I am endless, and the punishment which is given from my hand is endless punishment, for Endless is my name. Wherefore—Eternal Punishment is God's punishment. Endless punishment is God's punishment (D&C 19:6, 10–12). The adjectives "eternal" and "endless" refer to God, not to the punishment. I'm grateful for the restoration of this truth. Because of modern-day revelation, the Church understands that our postmortal estate is not permanent but a further step in our eternal progression, providing a time to prepare for the Resurrection, Judgment Day, and a subsequent assignment to one of three degrees of incomprehensible glory.

However, many Church members have the notion that the spirit world consists of only two realms, paradise or spirit prison. In reality, Church leaders have taught that there are multiple realms in the spirit world.

President Young suggested multiple spirit world "departments."[1] He also taught that spirits can progress from "department to department."[2]

At President Jedediah Grant's funeral (December 1856) President Heber C. Kimball quoted several things President Grant had told him about the spirit world (where he had spent two consecutive nights prior to his death). President Grant saw the spirits "organized in their several grades," and that he saw "grade after grade."[3]

Parley P. Pratt, speaking of the spirit world, said that there are "many levels of good and evil."[4]

This teaching is not exclusive to Church leaders. Emanuel Swedenborg also wrote of seeing three levels in "heaven."[5] Dr. Ritchie, who "died" in a military hospital, visited five postmortal "levels."[6] Apparently he was allowed to see the highest spirit world realm (or perhaps the celestial kingdom): "I can say that the Risen Christ, having conducted me through four realms of life after death, that in the highest realm [the fifth, but Benson would have called it the seventh], He showed me beings who were like Him when it came to the love, light, and life they put forth."[7]

The Spirit World Realms

In his research, Dr. Raymond Moody discovered that "those who are 'dead' for a longer period gain greater spirit world insight than those who are 'dead' for a shorter time."[8]

This being the case, Monsignor Robert Hugh Benson, who has inhabited a "department" in the spirit world since his death in 1914, would possess especially great knowledge and experience. You may wish to review the bibliographical synopsis of *Life in the World Unseen*. Benson proclaims that the spirit world is composed of seven spheres or realms, which he ranks in ascending order, the seventh sphere being the highest. These spheres are arranged in a band of concentric circles around the earth. They are not lighted by the sun but by the Light of Christ.[9] Each sphere has its resident ruler, but all rulers belong to a higher sphere than where they preside. He makes it clear that they preside, they do not rule.[10] Prerequisites to the calling are long tenure in the spirit world, great spirituality, a great deal of knowledge of (and experience in) the spirit world, exceptional kindness, and infinite patience.[11]

Benson said that spirits can progress to higher realms: "The high spheres are within the reach of every . . . soul."[12]

He continued, "Every spirit residing in the lower realms hates the unhappiness there." However, under God's direction, "great organizations exist to help every single soul who is living in them to rise out of them into the light."[13]

The plan of salvation and the Atonement are still in full effect (except in hell, where the inhabitants have apparently rejected the Atonement, at least for now). What marvelous hope this provides for those of us who fervently wish that deceased friends and relatives had more fully participated in God's plan while in mortality!

According to Benson, each sphere is completely invisible to the inhabitants of the spheres below it. In other words, the lower realms are unable to "see" the higher realms (unless invited and escorted), but the higher realms can see and even visit the lower realms. This can perhaps best be explained, in mortal terms, as the realms having different "frequencies."[14] (Perhaps the words "dimensions" or "planes of existence" could also apply.) There are many entry points into a realm.[15]

Benson taught that lower realms are partially divided according to their associated worldly nations and thus carry on many customs and even wear traditional dress, although it is actually a "replica" of earthly clothing.[16] However, as one develops spiritually and gains more knowledge and is thus qualified to progress into higher realms, these cultural and national distinctions disappear.

The majority of those who experience an NDE marvel at the meticulous organization of the spirit world.[17] Dr. Neal explained, "Each of us is like a small piece of thread that contributes to the weaving of a very large and very beautiful tapestry."[18]

Although not an NDEr himself, Dr. Moody's study of NDEs concludes that many NDEers return with a sense that everything in the universe is connected,[19] just as mortality is tightly correlated to the spirit world.

Duane Crowther, a renowned author of several Church books, quoted the succinct conclusion of one NDEer: "Everything has a reason. But you don't know that until you are on the other side."[20]

Elder Neal A. Maxwell stated, "There cannot be a grand plan of salvation for all mankind unless there is also a plan for each individual. The salvational sum will reflect all its parts."[21]

One's assigned realm is perfect and just for that individual. Betty Eadie expressed that "there are many levels of development, and we will always go to the level where we are most comfortable."[22]

It appears that most realms are a tremendous improvement from mortality. Benson told us only that he is not assigned to the highest nor to the lowest realms (he uses the plural, suggesting that there are at least two realms higher and at least two lower), but that his assigned realm is beautiful, glorious, and joyful beyond possible description. He explains that there are other realms "infinitely better—and infinitely worse."[23]

He also described his perception of how the great plan of salvation is applied in the spirit world: "There are other realms immeasurably more beautiful than that in which we [are] now happily living; realms of surpassing beauty into which we cannot penetrate until such time as we have earned the right to enter, either as visitors or as inhabitants. But though we may not pass into them, the glorious souls who dwell in them can come into realms of celestial rarity, and can visit us here."[24]

Benson called these visitors "perfect beings . . . [whose] beauteous souls have but to pass [by us] upon their way to fill us with such an ecstasy of spiritual exaltation as to remain with us for long after their return to their high estate."[25]

Just as the Lord assigns angels (and the angelic) in this life to help people progress, learn, and receive comfort, He apparently also utilizes angels to help His children who have transitioned to the spirit world to continue progressing.

Referring to the realms of the spirit world, I have found no one, other than Monsignor Benson, who has spoken of being assigned to a particular realm. This makes sense: all other NDEers were consigned, or chose, to return to earth, but not he. He died in 1914, at age forty-three, and journeyed to his assigned spirit world realm, where he still abides. *Life in the World Unseen* was published many earth-years after he died and began abiding in the spirit world. His sequel, *More About Life in the World Unseen* was published in the 1950s, about forty years after his death. His third book, *Here and Hereafter*, purports being dictated in 1957, and it was published in 1968. Considering the length of time since his transition to the spirit world, plus the character he demonstrates, I supposed that he would have attained a higher realm, yet he stated in the third book that "we know that when we pass into a higher realm, we shall be happier still. We have not yet enjoyed that experience."[26] It comforts me to know that this ultimate comment was published in 1968. It has been more than fifty years, and I hope such an impressive man now finds himself in a higher realm.

Benson taught us much about his realm and realm progression: "I do not suggest that we are in a state of perfection. We should be in an immensely higher realm if we were, but we are in perfection in so far as this realm is concerned. If we, as individuals, become more perfect than the realm in which we live, we, ipso facto, become worthy of advancing to a higher state, and we do so. But while we are where we are, we are living in a state of perfection according to the limits of that realm."[27]

Perhaps the perfection he alludes to is the great enjoyment and comfort of his postmortal life. While awaiting the start of a concert, he stated, "Never have I experienced such a feeling of real, genuine enjoyment as came upon me at this moment. I was in perfect health and perfect happiness, seated with two of the most delightful companions, Edwin and Ruth; unrestricted by time or weather, or even the bare thought of them; unhampered by every limitation that is common to our old incarnate life."[28]

The Realms

Before examining the particular realms, some terms require clarification. Hell is the lowest spirit world realm, and paradise is the highest. Between these are several departments (in Brigham Young's terminology) that constitute the spirit prison. As Benson and others have declared, some of these realms are magnificent. So why would they be referred to as prison?

I believe that every realm—except paradise and hell—is a "spirit prison" in that the inhabitants do not receive the fulness of truth, power, and responsibility associated with the highest realm, paradise.[29] Although the ambiance is different from realm to realm, all but those in the highest realm have limitations associated with the achieved realm, until they attain paradise. (Note again Benson's comment, "We are free agents in every sense of the term, within the confines of our own realm."[30])

Each realm has appointed messengers from a higher realm, who are "clothed with power and authority" to "go forth and carry the light of the gospel . . . to the spirits of all men" (D&C 138:30). The Savior's efforts to bring all mankind unto Him continue. In the spirit world, this is apparently accomplished individually and incrementally, progressing from lower realms to higher—and for those who will abide by the necessary irrevocable laws—to the highest. I personally believe that it is a blessing from a merciful God that the more wicked spirits will await the second resurrection. They will have the Millennium in which they may choose to make further progress before their final judgment.

Hell

This realm is frequently referred to scripturally as "the depths of hell." Its inhabitants have totally, over time, given themselves over to Satan, and, like one-third of God's premortal children, have completely rejected the Savior and His Atonement.

Of these, Nephi lamented that Satan had grasped them "with his awful chains, from whence there is no deliverance" (2 Nephi 28:22).

Like the last generation of Lehi's descendants (as well as the last of the Jaredites) they "suffer the sorrowing of the damned, because the Lord will not always suffer them to take happiness in sin" (Moroni 9:18), and "the Spirit hath ceased striving with them" (Ether 15:9; Moroni 8:28, 9:4).

In the Savior's parable of Lazarus and the rich man, Father Abraham informed the rich man, "Between us and you there is a great gulf fixed: so that they who would pass from hence you cannot; neither can they pass to us, that would come from hence" (Luke 16:26).

Benson taught, "There are many parts of the spirit world that are a thousand times worse than anything that can be found in the earth world."[31]

Recounting an escorted visit to hell, Benson explained, "[Their] dwellings were nothing more than mere hovels. They were distressing to gaze upon, but it was infinitely more distressing to contemplate that these were the fruits of men's lives upon earth."[32]

"Our nostrils were first assailed by the most foul odors, odors that reminded us of the corruption of flesh in the earth world" Ibid., 85).

Eben Alexander, a neurosurgeon, described the smell as "a little like feces, a little like blood, and a little like vomit."[33]

"Their bodies presented the outward appearance of the most hideous and repulsive malformations and distortions, the absolute reflection of their evil minds."[34]

Benson described one inhabitant as follows: "The hands were shaped like the talons of some bird of prey, with the finger nails so grown as to have become veritable claws. The face of this monster was barely human, so distorted was it, and malformed."[35]

He continued, "Their limbs were indescribably distorted and malformed, and in some cases their faces and heads had retrograded to the merest mockery of a human countenance. Others again we observed to be lying prone on the ground as though exhausted from undergoing torture, or because of expending their last remaining energy upon inflicting it, before they could gather renewed strength to recommence their barbarities."[36]

As this inhabitant had sown, so had he reaped. Benson explained, "Ugliness of mind and deed can produce nothing but ugliness."[37]

He continued, "The sounds were in keeping with the awful surroundings, from mad raucous laughter to the shriek of some soul in torment—inflicted by others as bad as himself."[38]

Several other people who experienced NDEs visited this miserable realm. Not surprisingly, these observers identified the inhabitants as "vassals of the devil,"[39] "horrific beings that clutch and claw at others,"[40] "hideous and grotesque,"[41] "savage, as in mortal life,"[42] and "intent upon evil."[43]

Dr. Ritchie called them "the most frustrated, the angriest, the most completely miserable I had ever laid eyes on."[44]

They live in a gloomy, barren, hostile place, in a total absence of love.[45] They still carry the addictions they acquired in the flesh.[46] locked in with their habits of hatred and lust.[47] Dr. Ritchie described sexual abuses being performed in feverish pantomime: "Perversions I had never dreamed of were being vainly attempted all around us, accompanied by howls of frustration."[48]

Elder Orson Pratt taught that these souls remain in hell "with the devil and his angels in torment and misery until the final end, then they come forth."[49]

That "coming forth" will be the last resurrection. Are they, post-millennium, given another opportunity to repent before their resurrection? There is no doctrine of which I am aware. May we never have reason to know.

A quick interjection concerning the Millennium. Benson hinted at it when he said, "The day will assuredly come when our two worlds will be closely interrelated, when communication between the two will be a commonplace of life, and then the great wealth of resources of the spirit world will be open to the earth world, to draw upon it for the benefit of the whole human race."[50]

Now, back to "hell." Because its inhabitants have rejected the Savior's pleading to repent that they may not suffer even as He (D&C 19:15), they must pay the "uttermost farthing" (Matthew 5:26) for their sins. When their debt is fully paid, I hope they may flee hell.

Not surprisingly, there is divine purpose even in these dreadful abodes. "They [are] given the chance to realize two very important facts. One, you can only kill the physical body, not the soul. Two, only love, not hate, can bring them and others to true happiness."[51] God does not forget them. In Ritchie's words, "That entire unhappy plain was hovered over by beings . . . of light."[52]

Other Low Realms

Benson informed us of the character of some of these lower realm inhabitants. Speaking of one who had been a "successful" businessman in mortality, Benson explained, "He had not thought of much else than his business, and he always considered that any means were justified in gaining his own ends, provided they were legal. He was ruthless in his dealings with all others, and he elevated efficiency to the level of a god. In his home all things—and all people—were subservient to him. He gave generously to charity where there was likely to accrue the greatest advantage and credit. . . . But from what Edwin [Benson's assigned guide] had been able to glean from his story, he had scarcely committed one decent, unselfish action in the whole of his life. His motive was always self-aggrandizement."[53]

Benson's description of hypocritical religious leaders reminds us of the Pharisees in the days of the Savior and of the Savior's comments to Joseph in the Sacred Grove: "There are those whose earthly lives have been spiritually hideous though outwardly sublime; whose religious profession designated by a Roman collar, has been taken for granted as being synonymous with spirituality of soul. Such people have been mocking God throughout their sanctimonious lives on earth where they lived with an empty show of holiness and goodness. Here they stand revealed for what they are. But the God they have mocked for so long does not punish. They punish themselves."[54]

Benson included an important caveat in this classification: "Never must it be supposed that those who, in the earth's judgment, had failed spiritually, are fallen low. Many such have not failed at all, but are, in point of fact, worthy souls whose fine reward awaits them here."[55]

He also said that in these realms "many people who, without doing any harm, had never, never done any good to a single mortal upon earth; . . . such souls constantly harped upon the theme that they had done no harm to anyone."[56]

Sister Sarah LaNelle Menet, who had an NDE, adds the following:

> I also learned a word that is used in the spirit world for which an equivalent in our language does not exist. The word is xoi-coi. Though I am not sure of the spelling, it is pronounced "x-oy koy." This word means "someone who doesn't do anything meaningful while of earth." This person doesn't progress, help others, or care. In a way, he or she just takes up space, doing nothing worthwhile. Unfortunately, I learned that there are lots of spirits who come to earth and become xoi-cois. They live to "party" and spend countless hours trying only to entertain themselves and satisfy their wants, which they will never fill because these pleasures are empty and have no lasting or eternal value. They do nothing to elevate mankind or contribute to the improvement of the world. Such contributions can be large or small because all do not have the same power to make a difference, but the important thing is to try. Even very small acts of kindness can make a big difference.[57]

What a strong testament that both faith and works are required for a higher realm: "What profit is it, my brethren, for a man to say he hath faith, and have not works? Can faith save him? Yea, a man may say, I will show thee I have faith without works; but I say, Show me thy faith without works, and I will show thee my faith by my works" (James 2:14–15).

As we would suppose, many of those who are venerated on earth are consigned to a low realm, or even to hell. Benson learned from Edwin [his guide] that "we should be appalled by the catalogue of names, well known in history, who were living deep down in these noxious regions—men who had perpetrated vile and wicked deeds in the name of holy religion, or for the furtherance of their own despicable, material ends."[58]

To this Benson added the caveat that there are those who were great in mortality and remain great in the spirit world (and would obviously abide in a higher realm). Abraham Lincoln is one of many who comes to my mind.

Benson warned us of the influence of these realms upon the mortal world: "From the dark realms you will have wars and strife, unrest and discontent; you will have literature that is a disgrace to so-called civilization, and music, even, that is an abomination of impure sounds, such sounds as would never exist for an instant of time in [the higher] realms."[59]

I think it appropriate to end our examination of the lower realms with another quote from Monsignor Benson: "There is no light in the lowest realms; no warmth, no vegetation, no beauty. But there is hope—hope that every soul there will progress. It is in the power of each soul to do so, and nothing stands in the way but himself. It may take countless thousands of years to raise himself one inch spiritually, but it is an inch in the right direction."[60]

Dante was wrong! There is no realm in which the inhabitants must abandon all hope. The Infinite Atonement is indeed infinite.

Before studying the higher realms, let's take a moment to study the dead who choose to remain on the earth, and to examine inter-realm travel.

"Ghosts"

Dr. Ritchie saw the dead who could no longer make physical contact with the earth but whose hearts were still here: "For where your treasure is, there will your heart be also" (Luke 12:34).

As examples of these spirits who remain in the earth realms, Dr. Ritchie tells of one female spirit who "asked another [mortal woman] for a cigarette, begged her in fact, as though she wanted it more than anything in the world."[61]

Of course, the mortals were completely unaware of these spirits. Ritchie saw a number of deceased spirits in a bar, trying to grasp drinks that frustratingly passed right through their hands. He also saw a very drunk mortal. The deceased spirits could briefly take possession of his body and partake of the drunken sensation.

Elder Parley P. Pratt spoke of these postmortal spirits: "Many spirits of the departed, who are unhappy, linger in lonely wretchedness about the earth, and in the air, and especially about their ancient homesteads, and the places rendered dear to them by the memory of former scenes."[62]

Sarah Menet explained, "Mischievous spirits are the ones that haunt houses, knock things over, and make noises. Righteous spirits are not involved in such practices."[63] Benson explains that many of these lingerers are seeking revenge.[64]

President Brigham Young taught that they torment and tempt us mortals, just like the one-third who premortally followed Satan.[65] In fact, Nephi differentiates the followers of Satan as "devils" and as "unclean spirits" twice in one verse (1 Nephi 11:31).

Heber Q. Hale, a stake president in Canada late in the nineteenth century, had an extended visit to the spirit world and was asked to speak about it in general conference. He taught: "These unrepentant spirits having still like all the rest, their free agency, and applying themselves to no useful or wholesome undertaking, seek pleasure about their old haunts and exult to the sin and wickedness of degenerate humanity. To this extent, they are tools of Satan. . . . These wicked and unrepentant spirits, as allies of Satan and his host, operate through willing mediums in the flesh. These three forces constitute an unholy trinity upon the earth and are responsible for all the sin, wickedness, distress and misery among men and nations."[66]

I have found no official doctrine about the future for these spirits. I hope that in time they see the failure and the futility of their efforts and choose to pass to their appropriate realms to participate in the plan of salvation. Benson suggests that most eventually come around to the futility of their efforts and leave the earth for their realm.[67]

Travel in the Spirit World

It appears that realm-to-realm travel requires an escort and that travel to a higher realm also requires either attaining that realm or an invitation from someone who inhabits that realm.

Benson's explanation of this travel will be of particular interest to members of the Church: "When those of a lower realm travel to a higher, it is always by authority, either vested in the traveler, or in some other person of a higher sphere, who will act as an escort. In the former case, such authority takes the form of symbols or signs that are given to the holder who will always, and upon every occasion receive—even unasked—every assistance he may need. Many of these symbols have the power in themselves of preserving the traveler from the overwhelming effects of the higher spiritual atmosphere."[68]

He further stated, "To visit the lower realms it is necessary—for one's own protection—[to be given] certain powers and symbols, of which Edwin told us he was in full possession."[69]

We shall examine this more fully in chapter 10.

The Higher Realms

You will remember that the higher realms minister to the lower. These assignments could be referred to as mission calls. Further, the higher the realm, the less associated "carry-over" from the physical earth. Ethnic and national origin, traditions, customs, and cultures become less significant.[70] Assignments are more demanding, which means that the spiritual and intellectual demands increase, fostering continuing progress. We will learn more of the spirit world assignments and labors in subsequent chapters.

There is increasing light and enhanced joy with progression to a higher realm: more peace, more love, more mutual respect, more brotherhood, more ministering to others, more reverence. There are numerous religious denominations extant at the various levels (but their chapels all have one thing in common: no associated cemetery). However, with each higher realm, there is more "unity of the faith" (Ephesians 4:13), so I would suppose that the variety of religions decreases at each higher realm. Perhaps ironically, Benson, a deceased clergyman, is highly critical of the churches and their creeds, and he blames these creeds for much of the misunderstanding new arrivals to the spirit world have to overcome. (Remember the Prophet Joseph Smith's strong criticism of religious creeds.)

In the orientation Benson gives to Roger, who was newly arrived in the spirit world, he spoke of two churches. Apparently referencing the Catholic Church and the Protestant denominations, he stated: "The first of the two . . . claims to be the one true Church, and infallible. . . . The second Church has no authority whatsoever. Within broad limits, . . . its members can think and believe as they like. Both those Churches take a particular interest in this world—a religious interest, of course. Neither knows what precisely to expect in the way of an after-life. An after-life there must be, naturally, but they suggest nothing that does not imply some description of an essentially religious life. In effect, it means that the earth life is the real material life, and the after-life is conducted upon holy lines of some sort. Certainly the whole atmosphere will be pious, and totally unlike what man has been accustomed to on earth. They are right in the latter; this life is totally unlike the earth life, but not in the way they mean."[71]

Benson further explained, "The earth has never been left high and dry, without someone to tell them about all this [the spirit world, its nature, and its functionality]. Latterly, the flow of revelation has increased, but you must remember that one of the greatest ecclesiastical establishments on earth has long ago decreed that all revelation ceased when the last of the apostles passed from the earth."[72]

We conclude Benson's short teachings about churches with what I will call his lamentation: "I too left behind me things which I had rather left undone. But by great good fortune I have been enabled to put them right; [but] not entirely right. . . . Where I spoke with vigour when I was on earth, I have since spoken with extra double-strength vigour to make up for it."[73]

Temples exist in several realms but are described more like our Conference Center—at least in the realms below the highest ones: "Instructors from higher realms come to edify and educate."[74] Of this instruction Benson said, "There would be revealed to us some idea—but only a very small idea—of the magnitude of the Great Mind—the Greatest Mind in the Universe—that upholds this and every other world."[75]

Paradise

In paradise, the highest spirit world realm, inhabitants are apparently free of the constraints associated with the other realms. It appears that their only "bondage" is the absence of their physical bodies (D&C 138:50). They are busy in the Lord's work and progressing toward godhood.

It appears that Satan has no influence there. Brigham Young taught, "If we are faithful to our religion, when we go into the spirit world, the fallen spirits—Lucifer and the third part of the heavenly hosts that came with him, and the spirits of wicked men who have dwelt upon this earth, the whole of them combined will have no influence over our spirits."[76]

Does this also apply to spirit prison? Apparently not. President Young continued, "All of the rest of the children of men are more or less subject to them [Satan's host, and his wicked followers] as they were while here in the flesh."[77] It appears to me that satanic influence attenuates through the realms from complete dominance in hell to no influence in paradise.

It also appears that the testing aspect of our existence is complete at death for those who attain paradise. Elder McConkie said, "All the faithful Saints, all those who have endured to the end, depart this life with the absolute guarantee of eternal life. . . . Those who have been true and faithful in this life will not fall by the wayside in the life to come."[78]

President Brigham Young said the following of his visit to paradise:

> I have had to exercise a great deal more faith to desire to live than I ever experienced in my whole life to live. The brightness and glory of the next apartment is inexpressible. It is not encumbered so that when we advance in years we have to be stubbing along and be careful lest we fall. We see our youth, even, frequently stubbing their toes and falling down. But yonder how different! They move with ease and like

> lightning. If we want to behold Jerusalem as it was in the days of the Savior; or if we want to see the Garden of Eden as it was when created, there we are, and we see it as it existed spiritually, for it was created spiritually and then temporally, and spiritually it still remains. And when there we may visit any city we please that exists upon its surface. If we wish to understand how they are living here on these western islands, or in China, we are there; in fact, we are like the light of the morning. . . . We have the Father to speak to us, Jesus to speak to us, and angels to speak to us and we shall enjoy the society of the just and the pure who are in the spirit world until the resurrection. . . . When we get through this state of being [earth life], to the next room, I may call it, we are not going to stop there. We shall go on, doing all the good we can, administering and officiating for all whom we are permitted to administer and officiate for, and then go on to the next, and to the next, and to the next, until the Lord shall crown all who have been faithful on this earth, and the work pertaining to this earth is finished, and the Savior, whom we have been helping, has completed His task, and the earth, with all things pertaining to it, is presented to the Father. Then these faithful ones will receive their blessings and crowns, and their inheritances will be set off to them and be given to them, and they will then go on, worlds upon worlds, increasing for ever and ever.[79]

In the spirit world Monsignor Benson visited higher realms, including the highest (paradise) under the tutelage of an escort. He related the following regarding inter-realm travel:

> Many of these symbols have the power in themselves of preserving the traveler from the overwhelming effects of the higher spiritual atmosphere. [For more about these symbols, refer to the subheading "Travel in the Spirit World" earlier in this chapter.] This latter would not damage the soul, of course, but a soul thus unprepared would find itself in much the same situation as upon the earth when one emerges into brilliant sunlight after a prolonged stay in complete darkness. But as in the case of the earthly sunshine one can, after a suitable lapse of time, become again perfectly at ease in the normal bright light. There is no such adaptability there. The "blinding" effect will be continuous to one of a lower state. But with a perfect dispensation, means are provided so that the visiting soul shall undergo no spiritual discomfort or unhappiness. And that is just what one might expect, since such visits are made for happy reasons, and not as tests of spiritual stamina and endurance.[80]

Benson also noted, "Personages from those realms have more than astonished me with the accuracy of their foreknowledge of events that were to take place upon the earth-plane" (ibid., 123), and "those wise beings in the higher realms are in possession of all knowledge of what is transpiring on earth."[81]

Referring to this difference of knowledge in high realms, Benson taught:

> There is . . . an enormous amount of things that are not told us not because they are deep secrets, but because we have much to learn first. The fact is, that with our necessarily limited knowledge and posers or comprehension, we should fail to understand them in our present state of advancement. It is like your school books. . . . You were obliged to start at the beginning. A peep at the end of them would reveal things far beyond your then capabilities, and so would convey no meaning whatsoever. We are in no different case here as regards innumerable problems or questions. So we jog along, and we find we are none the worse off for not knowing the answers. Everything fits in into its proper place in these lands, and none of us would be handicapped in our progression by lack of knowledge. The knowledge will be there at the right moment. In the meantime, there is no harm in our having as many discussions as we like among ourselves. . . . If it's possible for us to have light thrown upon them—subject to the limitations I have mentioned—then the light will come.[82]

Benson's instruction reminds me of two scriptures: (1) "And he received not of the fullness at first, but continued grace to grace, until he received a fullness (D&C 93:13), and (2) "For my thoughts are not your thoughts, neither are your ways my ways, saith the Lord. For as the heavens are higher than the earth, so are my ways higher than your ways, and my thoughts than your thoughts" (Isaiah 55: 8–9).

Dr. Ritchie, who was apparently shown paradise, described the inhabitants as "beings who had followed His teachings and were now [revitalized] into spiritual beings who were like Him when it came to love, light, and life."[83] Note the echoes of 1 John 3:2: "When he shall appear, we shall be like him" (see also Moroni 7:48; D&C 130:1–2).

Benson detailed his invitation (with two other spirits) to visit this highest realm. His description merits our attention. "There are two ways, and two ways only, of penetrating into these lofty states. The first is through our own spiritual development and progression; the second is by special invitation from some dweller in those regions."[84] Benson visited by invitation.

Benson described the host who invited him: "The illustrious personage . . . was known by sight to every soul in the realms of light. His wish was always treated as a command, and his word was law. . . . His kingdom is ruled by the great universal law of true affection. . . . He is the great living visible link between the Father, the Creator of the Universe, and His children."[85]

Benson's entourage arrived at "the most magnificent building that the mind could ever contemplate."[86] Passing though the corridors, they "were greeted by the most friendly and gracious beings."[87]

When they came into their host's presence, he "thanked the [escorts] for bringing us to him. . . . We drew close to the window, and we could see beneath us a bed of the most magnificent white roses, as pure white as a field of snow, and which exhaled an aroma as exalting as the blooms from which it came. White roses, our host told us, were the flowers he preferred above all others."[88] Benson continues:

> His hair seemed to be as of bright golden light. . . . He looked to be young, to be of eternal youthfulness, but we could feel the countless eons of time . . . that lay behind him. . . . When he spoke, his voice was sheer music, his laugh as a rippling of waters, but never did I think it possible for one individual to breathe forth such affection, such kindliness, such thoughtfulness and consideration; and never did I think it possible for one individual to possess such an immensity of knowledge as is possessed by this celestial king. One felt that, under the Father of Heaven, he held all knowledge and wisdom. . . . We felt perfectly at home, perfectly at ease with him . . . He spoke to each of us individually, displaying an exact acquaintance with all our concerns, collectively and individually. . . . Finally, he came to the reason for his invitation to us to visit him. [We] had visited the dark realms. . . . He thought that it would be in the nature of a pleasant contrast if we were to visit the highest realm. . . . And he had asked us to visit him in order to tell us himself that these realms, wherein we were now visiting, were within the reach of every soul that is born upon the earth-plane.[89]

The host concluded the visit "with a blessing upon us all, and with a smile of such affection, of such ineffable benignity, he bade us God-speed."[90]

One NDEer said, "God, in his nature, is much more forgiving, understanding, and just than we as humans are able to comprehend."[91]

Another person said, "The garden was extraordinarily beautiful, but everything paled in his presence."[92]

Eadie expressed that a brilliant light, brighter than the sun, radiated all around Him[93] and that "Jesus Christ is the only door through which we can return."[94]

A child said, "Jesus told me that he died on the cross so we could go see his dad."[95]

How well this child articulated the Savior's sacrifice that we might return to "my Father, and your Father" (John 20:17). If we are true and faithful, what a magnificent blessing it will be ours to, in the appointed time, shout praises to His name while in His presence.

Stated Dr. Ritchie, "This was the most totally male Being I had ever met. . . . This Person was power itself, older than time and yet more modern than anyone I had ever met. . . . This Presence was unconditional love. An astonishing love. A love beyond my wildest imagining. This love knew every unlovable thing about me . . . and accepted and loved me just the same."[96]

Ritchie also wrote, "There was mirth in the Presence beside me, now I was sure of it: the brightness seemed to vibrate and shimmer with a kind of holy laughter—not at me and my silliness, not a mocking laughter, but a mirth that seemed to say that in spite of all error and tragedy, joy was more lasting still."[97]

Benson also mentioned this mirth: "There would seem to be in some minds that the higher one's spiritual status becomes the more serious one has to be. Such a notion is entirely false. The reverse is the truth. Light-hearted merriment that comes truly from the heart, that hurts no one and is directed against no one to their detriment, but that is indulged in for the sake of making others merry, such merriment is welcomed and encouraged in the spirit world."[98]

I am grateful for these observations. Personally, paradise wouldn't be much fun without humor. Romain Gary, a French aviator, said "Humor is an affirmation of dignity, a declaration of man's superiority to all that befalls him."[99]

Many years ago, I had an opportunity to apply this principle. Soon after my graduation from Air Force pilot training, I attended a course that every Air Force aviator anticipated with dread. The intent of the course was to prepare us should we be captured by the enemy and become POWs. They did a "dreadfully" good job of simulating that experience. Several times I saw grown men cry. Toward the end of the course, when we were all exhausted by constant maltreatment, our "guards" transported us to terrain consisting of steep, rocky hills. We "POWs" all had heavy black hoods over our heads. We were lined up, and each of us required to put our hands on the shoulders of the man in front of us. They then marched us up and down these steep hills. It was miserable. Without vision, we were tripping all over each other. Many fell and rolled down the rocky hills, resulting in bumps and bruises. Each time a fellow POW fell, we were collectively punished. With our hands still on the shoulders of another, we were forced to double-time to the location of our fallen comrade. Of course, at the faster pace, coupled with increasing exhaustion, many more fell, and the guards increased the pace and misery of the ordeal. Though I couldn't see, the frustration and discouragement of our group was tangible. Remembering Gary's axiom, I hoped to raise the spirits of my classmates. I suddenly realized that with hoods over our heads and our constant movement, the guards would be unable to detect the source of any given voice. At the top of my lungs, I yodeled. I immediately heard several chuckles. The guards were infuriated, and threatened whoever was yodeling, but couldn't identify me as the source. I repeated my yodeling every few minutes, and the chuckling increased each time. Finally, the guards realized that their effort to "break" us with this procedure was futile and returned us to our "POW" camp. Even with the deck stacked against us in nearly every way, properly executed humor had given us a victory over our tormenters. Incidentally, airmen who were subsequently held as POWs commended the course for the preparation it provided.)

Allow me, for a moment, to completely deviate from the subject of this book to relate the final event of this course. We had suffered hunger, physical and mental fatigue, the cold, abuse, solitary confinement and more. We had just spent the entire night without sleep, performing enforced physical labor. The guards called us into formation, facing east, at the crack of dawn. We expected more maltreatment. Catching us by complete surprise, the guards completely abandoned their cruel but forged identity and raised "Old Glory," backlit by the rising sun, while at the same time, over the same loudspeaker that had fed us constant propaganda, playing the "Star-Spangled Banner." At that moment, almost every "grown man" in our class cried. God bless America.

NOTES

1. *Teachings of Presidents of the Church: Brigham Young*, 282.
2. Crowther, *Life Everlasting*, 175.

3. Cited in *Discipleship*, 107.
4. Crowther, 247.
5. Top, *Glimpses Beyond Death's Door*, 53.
   Emanuel Swedenborg, born in 1758, was a renowned Swedish theologian, scientist, and mystic. He claimed numerous revelations concerning the afterlife. Some fit so well with the Church's doctrine that enemies of the Church claimed that Joseph Smith plagiarized Swedenborg, just as some of them still push the now widely discredited theory that the Book of Mormon was plagiarized from a manuscript written by Solomon Spaulding. I have not read Swedenborg's work, but Brother and Sister Top reference it several times in their book *Glimpses Beyond Death's Door*.
6. Ritchie, *Return from Tomorrow*, 47; *Ordered to Return*, 45. I have previously included my synopsis of *Return from Tomorrow*, but to correlate Dr. Ritchie's two books I reiterate a portion. *Return from Tomorrow* essentially "opened the door" to lending credence to NDEs, and it has been an immensely popular best seller. It was first published in 1978. My copy, printed in 2004, was from the thirty-third printing.
   Ordered to Return is the follow-up book to *Return from Tomorrow* and provides a magnificent example of how an NDE can enhance one's life. Dr. Ritchie believes that his orientation to the spirit world was hosted by the Savior. Dr. Ritchie thereafter dedicated his life to advocating Christ and exhorting others to follow His example. As a follower of Christ, he has tried to especially serve the downtrodden. Although not a member of the Church, Ritchie mentions it twice. First, he uses some of the Church's three-degrees-of-glory nomenclature in describing the realms of the spirit world. Second, he states, "We all need to be ashamed of the way we treated our Mormon brothers and sisters when they began."
7. *Ordered to Return*, 173.
8. Moody, *Life after Death*, 18. This is one of three books by Dr. Moody. In this early scientific study of NDEs, Moody explores experiences that are common to many who have experienced an NDE, and he explains why they could not be conjured up by the throes of a dying brain. He expresses some of the weakness of science that inhibits its recognition of NDEs. Although Dr. Moody does not share his personal religious views, he refers favorably to "Mormons" several times in his three books.
9. Borgia, *Life in the World Unseen*, 128.
10. Borgia, *More About Life in the World Unseen*, 154.
11. Ibid., 129.
12. Ibid., 85.
13. Ibid.
14. Ibid., 130.
15. Ibid.
16. Borgia, *More About Life in the World Unseen*, 19.

17. Moody, *The Light Beyond*, 42; Ritchie, *Return from Tomorrow*, 14.
18. Neal, *To Heaven and Back*, 102.
19. Moody, *The Light Beyond*, 42.
20. Crowther, 58.
21. Maxwell, *But for a Small Moment*, 98.
22. Eadie, *Embraced by the Light*, 83.
23. Borgia, *Life in the World Unseen*, 54.
24. Ibid., 54, with echoes of D&C 138.
25. Ibid., 56.
26. Borgia, *Here and Hereafter*, 82.
27. Borgia, *Life in the World Unseen*, 69.
28. Ibid., 66.
29. Crowther, 275.
30. Ibid.
31. Borgia, *Life in the World Unseen*, 83.
32. Ibid, 82.
33. Alexander, *Proof of Heaven*, 55. Written by a neurosurgeon who, prior to his NDE, had lived a very analytical, materialistic life. From his NDE he recognizes the superiority of the spiritual body to the mortal body, particularly the immortal mind to the mortal brain. Though the book is about three-fourths "filler," it includes some well-expressed thoughts relative to the supreme importance of the spiritual aspects of life and of love.
34. Borgia, *Life in the World Unseen*, 86.
35. Ibid., 134.
36. Ibid., 136.
37. Ibid., 138.
38. Ibid., 86.
39. Top, 179.
40. Nelson, *Beyond the Veil*, 151.
41. Crowther, 126.
42. Ibid.
43. Young, 282.
44. Ritchie, *Return from Tomorrow*, 63.
45. Top, 167.
46. Ritchie, *Return from Tomorrow*, 38.
47. Ibid., 64.
48. Ibid.
49. Crowther, 279.
50. Borgia, *Life in the World Unseen*, 74.
51. Ritchie, *Return from Tomorrow*, 41.
52. Ibid., 66.
53. Borgia, *Life in the World Unseen*.
54. Ibid., 83.
55. Ibid.

56. Ibid.
57. Menet, *There Is No Death,* 98–99. Details Sarah Menet's NDE that came after a failed suicide attempt. It correlates very well with the NDEs of other people of character. As is occasionally granted to NDErs, she foresees some of the events that will precede the Second Coming. Her "visions" are uncannily similar to what others have reported seeing. These visionary experiences are not included in this book because of their speculative nature and because they are beyond this book's scope.
58. Ibid., 86.
59. Borgia, *Here and Hereafter,* 87.
60. Ibid.
61. Ritchie, *Return from Tomorrow,* 56.
62. Crowther, 236.
63. Menet, 121.
64. Borgia, *Here and Hereafter,* 40.
65. Young, 282.
66. Crowther, 238.
67. Borgia, *Here and Hereafter,* 40.
68. Borgia, *Life in the World Unseen*, 62.
69. Ibid., 61–62.
70. Top, 160.
71. Borgia, *More About Life in the World Unseen,* 50.
72. Ibid., 48–49.
73. Ibid., 49.
74. Borgia, *Life in the World Unseen*, 178.
75. Ibid., 90. Benson refers to "worlds" in the plural several times.
76. Young, 282.
77. Young, 283.
78. McConkie, "The Dead Who Die in the Lord."
79. Young, 282–83.
80. Borgia, *Life in the World Unseen*, 61–62.
81. Ibid., 183.
82. Borgia, *More About Life in the World Unseen,* 93.
83. Ritchie, *Ordered to Return,* 173.
84. Borgia, *Life in the World Unseen*, 188.
85. Ibid., 191.
86. Ibid., 194.
87. Ibid., 197.
88. Ibid., 198.
89. Ibid.
90. Ibid., 200.
91. Moody, *Reflections on Life After Life,* 178. Dr. Moody adds insights derived from additional research since writing *Life After Life.* Of interest to members of the Church, he says: "It is noteworthy that members of the Church of Jesus Christ of Latter-day Saints (the Mormons) have been aware of accounts

of near-death experiences for many years and circulate these stories among themselves." He apparently does not know that that is just the tip of the proverbial iceberg: the Church is certainly doing work in behalf of the dead that is unprecedented in any religion, at any time, Christian or otherwise.

92. Nelson, 760.
93. Eadie, 40.
94. Ibid., 85.
95. Burpo, *Heaven Is for Real,* 111. A cute book (and also a movie) about the NDE of a three-year-old boy, told in the purity and sincerity of a child. His father, a Christian minister, learns simple truths from his son's experiences that are in conflict with his theological training. For example, his son teaches him that the Trinity is composed of three distinct beings. The book contains a lot of filler material; the spirit world experiences comprise only about one-third of the book.
96. Ritchie, *Return from Tomorrow,* 49.
97. Ibid., 54.
98. Borgia, *Life in the World Unseen*, 190.
99. Romain Gary; see brainyquote.com/quotes/romain_gary_172688. Accessed May 8, 2020. I keep a quote book, and I first saw this R. Gary quote in *Reader's Digest* probably thirty years ago.

Chapter 10

TIME, SPACE, AND ENVIRONMENT

Now that we have a better sense for the people and places in the spirit world, let's look at how the dimensions of time and space are different there.

Time

Time exists in the spirit world, though it's very different from how mortals experience time. Moses "beheld the world upon which he was created; and Moses beheld the world and the end thereof, and all the children of men which are, and which were created" (Moses 1:8). The brother of Jared enjoyed a similar experience: "[God] showed unto the brother of Jared all the inhabitants of the earth which had been, and also all that would be; and he withheld them not from his sight, even unto the ends of the world" (Ether 3:25).

Elder Maxwell expressed that "we cannot fully understand time while we are inside of it."[1]

Obviously, Moses and the brother of Jared (and undoubtedly many others) "stepped out" of the constraints of time as we know them.

Those who have experienced an NDE are invariably challenged to describe time as it exists in the spirit world. After his NDE, Dr. Eben Alexander expressed, "Time in this place was different from the simple linear time we experience on earth and is as hopelessly difficult to describe as every other aspect of it."[2]

When asked how long she had been in the spirit world, one NDEr replied, "It could have been a minute, or 10,000 years."[3]

Other NDErs expressed time in the spirit world as "changed, compounded, absent,"[4] or "compressed."[5] It is certainly less constraining than in mortality.

Emanuel Swedenborg stated that "time and space no longer pose the obstacles they do in physical life."[6]

Dr. Ritchie said concerning his NDE that "it would have taken weeks of ordinary time even to glance at so many events, yet I had no sense of minutes passing."[7] Ritchie "died" in a military hospital where careful records were kept. The log shows that he was dead for only nine minutes.[8]

Joseph Smith spoke of the angels who dwell among the Gods: "All things for their glory are manifest, past, present, and future, and are continually before the Lord" (D&C 130:7).

C. S. Lewis, a respected and devout Christian theologian and author, said it this way: "But suppose God is outside and above the Time-line. In that case, what we call 'tomorrow' is visible to Him in just the same way as what we call 'today.' All the days are 'Now' for Him. He does not remember you doing things yesterday; He simply sees you doing them, because, though you have lost yesterday, He has not.

"He does not 'foresee' you doing things tomorrow; He simply sees you doing them; because, though tomorrow is not yet there for you, it is for Him."[9]

As we members of the Church serve as proxies for the dead in temples, we often express, "He [or she] has waited a long time for this ordinance." It appears that the nature of time in the spirit world renders this conclusion overly simplistic. Perhaps it would be more accurate to say, "It has been many earth years since he [or she] lived," because he or she now lives outside of "time" as we experience it.

The very articulate Monsignor Benson explains both time and space in the spirit world, attempting to give us the best understanding possible while we are yet confined to the "time" and "space" of mortality: "It is commonly thought by people of the earth-plane that in the spirit world time and space do not exist. That is wrong. We have both, but our conception of them differs from that of the earth world. . . . We have no clocks. . . . We have no recurrent seasons, no alterations of light and darkness or external indicators of time, and, in addition, we have no personal reminder, common to the incarnate, of hunger and thirst and fatigue [and] aging. . . . When we look forward to the arrival of a relative or friend into the spirit world it is towards the event that we cast our minds, not the year in which the event is to take place."[10]

Rachel's Experience

I often recall my experience with the afterlife as a single event—visiting with Gram—but I also communicated with others, including my maternal grandfather and my future children. This causes me to wonder if such communications were at separate times. My visit to the spirit world seemed brief, only a matter of seconds, yet it seems impossible to have communicated with so many and obtained such a high and clear level of understanding in such a short amount of time. Clearly, time in the spirit world is different from time in mortality. The Prophet Joseph Smith explained the passage of time in heaven best: "If you could gaze into heaven for five minutes, you would know more on a topic than if you studied it all of your life."[11] My visit to the spirit world could not have been longer that ten (earthly) days, but the vastness of information and understanding gained in that short time far exceeds mortal comprehension.

Space

Concerning space, Monsignor Benson taught, "Space must exist in the spirit world. Take my own realm alone, as an example. Standing at the window of one of the upper rooms of my house I can see across huge distances whereon are many houses and grand buildings. In the distance I can see the city with many more great buildings. Dispensed throughout the whole wide prospect are woods and meadows, rivers and streams, just as these occupy space in the earth world."[12]

Perhaps the best way to understand the vastness and the environment of the spirit world is to take a tour. Let's examine what Benson saw when he was given a tour.

A Visit to the City

Soon after Benson's arrival in the spirit world, his guide offered him a tour of a nearby city. Benson was not anxious to go. He said, "My mind had reverted to the narrow streets and crowded pavements of the earth; the buildings huddled together because space is so valuable and costly;

the heavy, tainted air, made worse by streams of traffic; I had thought of hurry and turmoil, and all the restlessness of commercial life and the excitement of passing pleasure."[13]

What a pleasant surprise awaited him: "I had no conception of a city of eternal beauty, as far removed from an earthly city as the light of day is from black night. Here were the broad thoroughfares of emerald green lawns in perfect cultivation, radiating, like the spokes of a wheel, from a central building which, as we could see, was the hub of the whole city. There was a shaft of pure light descending upon the dome of this building, and we felt instinctively—without Edwin [the guide] having to tell us—that in this temple we could together send up our thanks to the Great Source of all, and that there we should find none other than the Glory of God in Truth."[14]

As to the city's purpose, Monsignor Benson explained, "The city was devoted to the pursuit of learning, to the study and practice of the arts, and to the pleasures of all in this realm. It was exclusive to none, but free for all to enjoy with equal right. Here it was possible to carry on so many of those pleasant fruitful occupations which had been denied them, for a variety of reasons, [perhaps, such as being born during the Dark Ages] whilst they were incarnate."[15]

We will spend some time "touring" the city. It teaches much about the realm in which Benson resides.

There was not a single dark location in the city. The light radiating from God filled every corner and crevasse.

While in the city, they visited a great hall dedicated to the art of painting: "This hall was of very great size and contained a long gallery, on the walls of which were hanging every great masterpiece known to man. They were arranged in such a way that every step of earthly progress could be followed in proper order, beginning with the earliest times and so continuing down to the present day. Every style of painting was represented, gathered from all parts of the earth. It must not be thought that such a collection, as we were now viewing, is only of interest and service to people who have a full appreciation and understanding of the painter's art. Such could not be further from the case."[16]

He continued, "There were groups listening to the words of able teachers, who were demonstrating the various phases in the history of art as exemplified upon the walls, and they were, at the same time giving such a clear and interesting position that none could fail to understand."[17]

Concerning the quality of the artwork, Benson expressed the following:

> A number of the pictures I recognized as I had seen their "originals" in the earth's galleries. Ruth [a recently deceased woman also under the tutelage of Edwin] and I were astonished when Edwin told us that what we had seen in those galleries were not the originals at all. We were now seeing the originals for the first time. What we had seen was an earthly counterpart, which was perishable from the usual causes—for example, from fire or the general disintegration through the passage of time. But here we were viewing the direct results of the thoughts of the painter, created in the etheric before he actually transferred those thoughts to his earthly canvas. It could be plainly observed, in many cases, where the earthly picture fell short of that which the painter had in his mind. He had endeavored to reproduce the exact conception, but through physical limitations this exact concept had eluded him. In some instances, it had been the pigments that had been to fault when, in the early times, the artist had been unable to procure or evolve the particular shade of color he wanted. But though he lacked physically, his mind had known precisely what he wished to do. He had built it up in the spirit—the results of which we were now able to see—while he had failed to do so on the material canvas.[18]

Benson said that it was impossible to convey to mortals the paramount difference: "These pictures were alive. . . . They were never flat. . . . The subject stood out almost as though it were a model . . . The colors glowed with life, even among the very early works."[19]

This leads to an important aspect of at least the middle and higher realms: universal animation. Everything is "living," or in other words, contains life. Benson clarified that nothing there is inert; everything is animate.[20] Gems shine from within, rather than reflecting light.[21]

This animation comes from what Benson calls "The Source."[22] He provided an example: "A recently deceased young man is interested in horticulture, particularly flowers. He tries his hand at spirit world flower creation. He has to learn much to organize a beautiful flower, but when he succeeds, the flower must be animated. A request is sent to the highest realms, and 'spirit' is instilled into the flower. From that time, it possesses life and radiates beauty, fragrance, and joyous praising of God."[23]

As Benson well illustrated, in at least the higher realms of the spirit world everything is "alive," or animated, but many things do not have will. The flower provides an excellent example. It is filled with joy and love for God and receives joy by sharing its beauty and fragrance with others, but it is perfectly content to be a flower. It has no will to be anything else or anywhere else.

Benson's next example could well be called "living waters":

> My friend quite calmly walked into the lake until he was thoroughly immersed, and the two of us followed his example.
>
> What I was expecting to result from this I cannot say. At least I anticipated the customary effect of water upon one in similar circumstances on earth. Great, then was my surprise—and my relief—when I discovered that the water felt more like a warm cloak thrown round me than the penetration of liquid. The magnetic effect of the water was of like nature to the brook into which I had thrust my hand, but here the revivifying force enveloped the whole body, pouring new life into it. It was delightfully warm and completely buoyant. It was possible to stand upright in it, to float upon it, and of course, to sink completely beneath the surface of it without the least discomfort or danger. Had I paused to think I might have known that the latter was inevitably bound to be the case. The spirit is indestructible. But beyond this magnetic influence there was an added assurance that came from the water, and that was its essential friendliness, if I may so call it. It is not easy to convey any idea of this fundamentally spiritual experience. That the water was living one could have no doubt. It breathed its very goodness by its contact, and extended it heavenly influence individually to all who came within it. For myself, I experienced a spiritual exaltation, as well as a vital regeneration, to such an extent that I quite forgot my initial hesitancy and the fact that I was fully clothed. The latter now presented a perfectly natural situation, and this was further enhanced by my observing my two companions. My old friend, of course, was perfectly used to the water, and our new friend seemed to have accommodated herself rapidly to new usages.
>
> My mind was saved further perturbation when I recalled that as I withdrew my hand from the brook the water ran off of it, leaving it quite dry. I was already prepared, then, for what ensued as we came out of the lake. As I emerged the water merely ran away, leaving my clothes just as they were before. It had penetrated the material just as air or atmosphere on earth will do, but it had left no visible or palpable effect whatever. We and our clothes were perfectly dry!
>
> And now another word about the water. It was as clear as crystal, and the light was reflected back in every ripple and tiny wave in almost dazzlingly bright colors. It was unbelievably soft to the touch, and it buoyancy was of the same nature as the atmosphere, that is to say, it

> supported whatever was on it, or in it. As it is impossible to fall here by accident, as one does on earth, so it is impossible to sink in the water. All our movements are in direct response to our minds, and we cannot come to harm or suffer accident. It is, I am afraid rather difficult to give a description of some of these things without going beyond the range of earthly minds and experience.[24]

For additional understanding of this concept, refer to Moses 3:5 and Doctrine and Covenants 138:56.

Now, let's return to Benson's tour of the spirit world city: "There were rooms wherein students of art could learn all that there is to be learned."[25] In fact, it was intimidating for Monsignor Benson. "Standing with all this enormous wealth of knowledge about us, I was staggered at my own ignorance.[26]

However, Edwin reassured him [and Ruth] "by telling us that we must not let the sight of so much knowledge frighten us, as we have the whole of eternity before us."[27] (For additional information about teachers in the spirit world, refer to chapter 13.)

The three of them subsequently visited the hall of literature, with equally astounding results: "Edwin led us into one spacious apartment which contained the histories of all the nations upon the earth-plane. To anyone who has a knowledge of earthly history, the volumes with which the shelves of this section of the great library were filled, would prove illuminating. The reader would be able to gain, for the first time, the truth about the history of his country. Every word contained in these books was the literal truth. Concealment is impossible, because nothing but the truth can enter these realms."

Benson recounted his experience with spirit world libraries:

> I have since returned to the library and spent much profitable time among its countless books. In particular I have dipped into history, and I was amazed when I started to read. I naturally expected to find that history would be treated in the manner with which we are all familiar, but with the essential difference that now I should be presented with the truth of all historical acts and events. The latter I soon discovered to be the case, but I made another discovery that for the first moment left me astounded. I found that side by side with the statements of pure fact of every act of persons of historical note, by statesmen in whose hands was the government of their countries, by kings who were at the head of those same countries, side by side with such statements was

> the blunt naked truth of each and every motive governing or underlying their numerous acts—the truth beyond disputation. Many of such motives were elevated, many, many of them were utterly base; many were misconstrued, many distorted. Written indelibly upon these spirit annals were the true narratives of thousands upon thousands of human beings, who, whilst upon their earthly journey, had been active participants in the affairs of their country. Some were victims to others' treachery and baseness; some were the cause or origin of that treachery and baseness. None was spared, none omitted. It was all there for all to see—the truth, with nothing extenuated, nothing suppressed.[28]

He added, "Although these books witness against the perpetrators of so many dark deeds in the world's history, they also bore witness to many deeds both great and noble."[29]

The angel Moroni warned Joseph Smith that his name "should be had for good and evil among all nations, kindreds, and tongues" (Joseph Smith—History 1:33). He endured being "had for evil" from the tender age of fourteen. He was continuously persecuted and acrimoniously denounced. Even many Saints that he had tutored at his feet turned against him, for at least a time, and joined in the critical clamor. Shortly before his death, he lamented, "You never knew my heart." As Benson taught, the day will come that the Prophet will be eternally vindicated.

Concluding the visit to the history library, Benson stated, "I also delved into church history, and the revelations I received in that direction were no better than those in the political sphere. They were, in fact, worse, considering in whose Name so many diabolical deeds were committed by men who, outwardly professing to serve God, were but instruments of men as base as themselves."[30]

George Ritchie's Perspective

Dr. George Ritchie was probably the first person to write a best seller about a personal NDE (*Return from Tomorrow*). Whereas Monsignor Benson's interests and talents were in the humanities (he authored numerous books and plays) Ritchie majored in chemistry and physics. It's not surprising that Benson went into great detail about the arts and history, while Ritchie was fascinated by science and was a man of much fewer words.

Like Benson, Ritchie declared that all things were created spiritually before their physical existence upon the earth. He wrote: "Why is it that inventors in different parts of the earth come up with the same ideas about the same time—Ford in America, Bentley in England, Peugeot in France? I believe I was shown the place where those who have already gone before us are doing research and want to help us when we begin to seriously search and turn deep within for answers."[31]

Ritchie declared that "the library [or research facility] in this realm was 'bigger than all the buildings in downtown Washington DC, put together."[32]

He visited a building "crowded with technological machinery."[33] The researchers were generally continuing in the same area of study they pursued in mortality, striving for the goal of improving the universe. They "were using instruments I had never seen and could not begin to understand. Not only could I not understand their instruments, I could not begin to comprehend their advanced technical thinking."[34]

"I'd prided myself a little on the beginning of a scientific education . . . but if these were scientific activities of some kind, they were so far beyond anything I knew, that I couldn't even guess what field they were in . . . some vast experiment was being pursued, perhaps dozens and dozens of such experiments."[35]

Concerning spirit world technology, Benson said, "All of the major discoveries that are of service to the earth-plane have come and will always come, from the spirit world."[36]

He elucidated "a mere hint to an earthly scientist is enough to set him upon the track of a dozen or more other discoveries. All that the scientists here are concerned with is the initial discovery, and in most cases the rest will follow."[37]

Ritchie added, "I understood that their work was motivated by sincere interest in what they were learning and a desire to help make the universe a better place to live, not money or fame. They were so far advanced in so many ways that it would be like taking my son, when he was six years of age, to one of the research laboratories at the University of Virginia and expecting him to comprehend what he was seeing."[38]

In these realms, one can choose to read a book or to absorb its content very quickly by telepathy. None of the students or researchers sought attention or recognition; they would not inhabit such a high realm if they possessed such motives.

As previously noted, Dr. Ritchie described the scientific side of the realm, while Monsignor Benson, with more of an arts background, focused on the beautiful music and works of art. Benson was humbled by the inexhaustible knowledge available, compared to his comparatively very limited knowledge, although he had been a man of many letters.

Whereas Ritchie refers to these resources as "libraries" or "research laboratories," Benson declared, "They are temples, rather, in which we spirit people are conscious of the eternal thanks that we owe to the Great Father for giving such unbounded happiness in a land of which so many upon the earth deny the reality."[39]

Benson also explained that there is no need for skyscrapers because spirit world space is unlimited.[40] You will remember that Elder Neal A. Maxwell taught that one of the characteristics of the spirit world is "vastness."[41]

However, the vastness of the spirit world does not burden inhabitants with the rigors of travel. Explained Benson, "I know I can travel uninterruptedly through enormous areas of space, areas far greater than the whole of the earth area trebled in size, or greater. I have not yet transversed anything like one fraction of the full extent of my own realm, but I am free to do so."[42]

Benson provided us a hypothetical example: "We decide to walk through the gardens and woods. The house is some 'distance' away, but that does not matter, because we never suffer from 'physical' fatigue and we are not otherwise engaged. We walk along together, talking happily, and after a certain lapse of 'time' we arrive at the house of our friend, and we have covered the intervening space on foot. On the journey from my house to the library I overcame the distance in between, and I dispensed with time for the occasion. On the way back I experienced an intuitive apprehension of time by walking slowly, and I restored a perception of distance to my mind by moving upon the solid ground and grassy fields of this realm."[43]

NOTES

1. Maxwell, *The Promise of Discipleship*, 83.
2. Alexander, *Proof of Heaven*, 67.
3. Moody, *Reflections on Life after Death*, 215.
4. Top, *Glimpses Beyond Death's Door*, 127.
5. Moody, *The Light Beyond*, 17.
6. Moody, *Life after Death*, 91.
7. Ritchie, *Return from Tomorrow* 51.
8. Ibid., 79.
9. Lewis, *Mere Christianity* 135.

10. Borgia, *Life in the World Unseen,* 120–24.
11. *Teachings of Presidents of the Church—Joseph Smith*, 419.
12. Borgia, *Life in the World Unseen,* 124.
13. Ibid., 43.
14. Ibid.
15. Ibid., 44.
16. Ibid.
17. Ibid.
18. Ibid., 44–45.
19. Ibid.
20. Borgia, *More About Life in the World Unseen*, 21; 65.
21. Ibid., 149.
22. Ibid., 107.
23. Ibid., 107–9.
24. Ibid., 28–29.
25. Ibid., 46.
26. Borgia, *Life in the World Unseen,* 49.
27. Ibid.
28. Ibid., 46–47.
29. Ibid., 48.
30. Ibid., 47; see also Joseph Smith—History 1:19.
31. Ritchie, *Ordered to Return,* 44.
32. Ibid.
33. Ritchie, *Ordered to Return,* 71.
34. Ibid., 43.
35. Ibid., 69–70.
36. Borgia, *Life in the World Unseen,* 185.
37. Borgia, *More About Life in the World Unseen,* 75.
38. Ibid., 43.
39. Borgia, *Life in the World Unseen,* 51.
40. Borgia, *More About Life in the World Unseen,* 73.
41. Maxwell, 105.
42. Borgia, *Life in the World Unseen,* 124.
43. Ibid., 125.

Chapter 11
MUSIC AND COLOR

Many who have experienced the spirit world remark on the indescribably beautiful music there.[1] Benson stated that music is a vital element of the spirit world[2] and that it greatly enhances one's joy.[3] He added, "The whole attitude to music held by so many people on the earth undergoes a great change when they eventually come to spirit. Music is looked upon by many on the earth-plane as merely a pleasant diversion, a pleasant adjunct to the earthly life, but by no means a necessity. Here it is part of our life, not because we make it so, because it is part of natural existence, as are flowers and trees, grass and water, and hills and dales. It is an element of our spiritual nature."[4]

In continuation of this theme, let's return to Benson's tour of a city soon after his arrival in the spirit world: "When I was on earth I never considered myself a musician, in an active sense, but I appreciated the art without very much understanding it. . . . Most of what I saw in the hall of music was new to me, and a great deal of it very technical. I have since added appreciably to my small knowledge, because I found that the greater the knowledge of music the more it helped one to understand so many things of life here, where music plays so important a part."[5]

He continued:

> The hall of music followed the same broad system as the other halls of the arts. The library contained books dealing with music as well as the scores of vast quantities of music that had been written on earth by composers who had now passed into spirit, or those who were still upon the earth. What are

> called on earth "master works" were fully represented among the musical scores upon the shelves, and I was interested to learn that there was hardly a work that had not since been altered by the composer himself since coming into the spirit. . . . As before, the library provided a complete history of music from the very earliest times, and those who were able to read music—not necessarily instrumentally, but with a familiarity of what the printed notes indicated—were able to see the great strides that the art had made during the ages. . . . Also contained in the library were so many of those books and musical works that have long since disappeared from earthly sight, or else are very scarce and so beyond the reach of many folk. The musical antiquary will find all those things that he had sighed for on earth, but which have been denied him, and here he can consult, freely, works that, because of their preciousness, would never be allowed into his hands on earth.[6]

Music Lessons

Benson said the following of music lessons:

> Many apartments were set aside for students who can learn of music in every branch, from theory to practice, under teachers whose names are known the world over. Some there are, perhaps, that would think that such famous people would not give their time to teaching the simple forms of music to simple lovers of music. But it must be remembered, as with the painters, composers have a different appraisement of the fruits of their brains after passing into spirit. In common with us all here, they see things exactly as they are—including their compositions. They find, too, that the music of the spirit world is very different in outward results from music performed on earth. Hence they discover that their musical knowledge must undergo sweeping changes in many cases before they can begin to express themselves musically. There are laws of music here which have no application to the earth whatsoever, because the earth is neither sufficiently progressed on the one hand, and on the other because the spirit world is of spirit, while the earth world is of matter. It is doubtful if the earth-plane will ever become ethereal enough to hear many of the forms of spirit music in the highest realms.[7]

Musical Instruments

Benson continued: "The many types of musical instrument so familiar on earth were to be seen in the college of music, where students could be taught to play on them. . . . As students acquire a mastery over their instrument they can join one of the many orchestras that exist here, or they can limit their performance to their many friends. It is not by any means surprising that many prefer the former because they can help to produce, in concert with their fellow musicians, the tangible effects of music upon a larger scale when so many more can enjoy such effects. . . . We were extremely interested in the many instruments that have no counterpart upon the earth-plane. They are, for the most part, specially adapted to the forms of music that are exclusive to the spirit world, and they are for that reason very much more elaborate."[8]

The Concert

Benson further explained, "Edwin [the guide] suggested to us that we might like to hear a concert of the spirit world. . . . The orchestra was composed of some two hundred musicians, who were playing on instruments that are well-known to earth, so that I was able to appreciate what I heard. As soon as the music began I could hear a remarkable difference from what I had been accustomed to hear on the earth-plane. The actual sounds made by the various instruments were easily recognizable as of old, but the quality of tone was immeasurably purer, and the balance and blend were perfect."[9]

Color

As one might expect, spirit world color is greatly amplified and purified, and has a broader spectrum. Sister Eadie described her visit to a garden: "I walked on the grass for a time. It was crisp, cool, and brilliant green, and it felt alive under my feet. But what filled me with awe in the garden more than anything were the intense colors. We have nothing like them. When light strikes an object here, the light reflects off that object in a certain color. Thousands of shades are possible. Light in the spirit world doesn't necessarily reflect off anything. It comes from within and appears to be a living essence. A million, a billion colors are possible."[10]

The Correlation of Music and Color

Not only are music and colors greatly improved from our "dreary" plane, but Benson proclaims that they are one and the same. He states, "Color and sound—that is, musical sound—are interchangeable terms in the spirit world. To perform some act that will produce color is also to produce a musical sound."[11]

Early in his spirit world experience, Benson noted the flowers: "There was another astonishing feature I noticed when I drew near to them, and that was the sound of music that enveloped them, making such soft harmonies as corresponded exactly and perfectly with the gorgeous colors of the flowers themselves."[12]

Of water, he wrote, "The water that sparkles and flashes colors is also creating musical sounds of purity and beauty. . . . The sounds are in perfect accord with the colors . . . and the perfect combination of both sight and sound is perfect harmony."[13]

Dr. Eben Alexander substantiated: "Seeing and hearing were not separate." He could hear the visual beauty of flowers, bodies of water, scenery, and even people.[14]

Color and the Concert

For a dynamic illustration of the color–music relationship, let's return with Monsignor Benson to the concert:

> The opening movement was of a subdued nature as regards its volume and sound, and we noticed that the instant the music commenced a bright light seemed to rise up from the direction of the orchestra until it floated, in a flat surface, level with the topmost seats, where it remained as an iridescent cover to the whole amphitheater. As the music proceeded this broad sheet of light grew in strength and density, forming as it were, a firm foundation for what was to follow. . . . Presently, at equal spaces round the circumference of the theater, four towers of light shot up into the sky in long tapering pinnacles of luminosity. . . . In the meanwhile, the central area of light had thickened still more, and was beginning to rise slowly in the shape of an immense dome covering the whole theater . . . the most delicate colors were diffused throughout the whole of the etheric structure. . . . The music was still being played, and in response to it the whole coloring of the dome changed, first to one shade, then to another, and many times a delicate blend of a number of shades according to the variation in theme or movement of the music. . . . It is difficult to give any adequate idea of the beauty of this wonderful musical structure. . . . . Unlike the earth where music can only be heard, there we had both heard and seen it.[15]

Musical Architecture

Benson explained, "The expert musician can plan his compositions by his knowledge of what forms the various harmonic and melodic sounds will produce. He can, in effect, build magnificent edifices upon his manuscript of music, knowing full well exactly what the result will be when the music is played or sung. By careful adjustment of his themes and his harmonies, the length of the work, and its various forms of expression, he can build a majestic form as grand as a Gothic cathedral. This is, in itself, a delightful part of the musical art in spirit, and it is regarded as musical architecture. The student will not only study music acoustically, but he will learn to build it architecturally, and the latter is one of the most absorbing and fascinating studies."[16]

NOTES

1. Moody, *Life after Life,* 46.
2. Borgia, *Life in the World Unseen,* 62.
3. Ibid., 63.
4. Ibid., 69.
5. Ibid., 63.
6. Ibid., 63–64.
7. Ibid., 64.
8. Ibid., 64–65.
9. Ibid., 66.
10. Eadie, *Embraced by the Light,* 78–79.
11. Borgia, 111.
12. Ibid., 13.
13. Ibid., 69.
14. Alexander, *Proof of Heaven,* 75.
15. Borgia, 67–68.
16. Ibid., 68–69.

Chapter 12

HOW AN NDE AFFECTS THE REST OF MORTAL LIFE

Thus far we have looked at what NDE experiences have taught us about the spirit world. But what about this world? How do experiences in the spirit world affect how a person views his or her continuing mortality?

Through his extensive study of NDEs, Dr. Ring found that most NDErs express that their experience was "the most important thing that ever happened to me."[1]

For example, the fear of death is generally gone. Brent and Wendy Top quoted Dr. Cherie Sutherland, an Australian near-death researcher: "Over three-quarters of my respondents said that they had a fear of death before the NDE, whereas not one person among my samples has a fear of death now."[2]

Dr. Moody stated matter-of-factly, "NDEers no longer fear death."[3]

Dr. Ring substantiates the same, and he concludes from his research that that fear never returns.[4]

Dr. George Moody added, "Most of the NDEers that I have met are mentally healthier than before the experience."[5]

Some NDEers have expressed that there is a great "thirst for knowledge" in the spirit world and that same "spirit of thirst" for knowledge remains with them after the experience.[6] Don't forget that notion—we will discuss this more in chapter 13.

Many expressed that since their NDE, they have an enhanced ability to sense needs in other individuals' lives.[7] They commonly express that one cannot fully understand this life until catching a glimpse of what lies beyond it.[8] Dr. Moody said, "They have all reported that their religious beliefs were strengthened."[9] He added, "It leads [them] to want to follow religious teachings."[10]

Dr. Ritchie stated, "I know that ever since the experience, I have carried a terrific sense of urgency to share it with the lonely, discouraged and diseased [sic] people such as alcoholics, drug addicts, and the social outcast."[11]

Dr. Neal said of her experience, "Taking a journey to heaven and back transformed my faith into knowledge and my hope into reality."[12]

Dr. Moody offered the example of a woman who faces a particularly challenging life but because of her NDE, "her attitude is one of luminous serenity."[13]

The NDEers that I have personally known all have an amazing peace about them, even in tremendously challenging times. The Savior said, "A good tree cannot bring forth evil fruit, neither can a corrupt tree bring forth good fruit. . . . Wherefore, by their fruits ye shall know them" (Matthew 7:18, 20). The evidence is clear: an NDE makes a person better and therefore must come from "a good tree."

Dr. Eben Alexander, after his recovery from illness and his return to performing brain surgeries, was so changed in his regard for, and tenderness toward others, that one of his coworkers jokingly asked him, "Are you Eben's twin brother, or what?"[14]

I conclude this segment with another statement by Dr. Rebecca Neal: "The absolute knowledge that God is real, that He has a plan for each of us, and that there really is life after death changes the way I experience each day. I do not fear death, and that also changes the way I experience the death of others, even my own son. I know that every day really does matter and that I need to be about God's business every day. I also know that God loves all people deeply and unconditionally . . . even those people whom I may not like or agree with. It motivates me to try to see the beauty in them that God sees."[15]

Rachel's Experience

I believe that life's purposes are magnified with each blessing or trial we experience. Further, my mortal life was significantly affected by my NDE. I have selected the three greatest:

- *The temporary nature of mortality.*
- *The ability of direct communication with Heavenly Father.*
- *Knowledge of life after death.*

I have gained a deep respect or reverence for my time here upon the earth because of my NDE. I now pay particular attention to the limited time I have as a mortal being. An ever-loving Father is over all, and life spent in mortality is according to His will. I now better recognize how the purpose of my earthly life is a part of the plan of salvation. I am aware that death can come anytime, anywhere, with no permission, and how easily it is to pass through the veil. Yet, I feel blessed with the comfort and peace the Holy Ghost provides.

My NDE has also affected my mortal life in that I know direct communication with my eternal Father in Heaven is possible through Jesus Christ. I value the importance of feeling or sensing the meaning of what I am struggling to relay to my Father in Heaven, rather than the use of words to solely communicate. Gram's message was transferred to me spiritually through the Holy Ghost, making comprehension utterly clear. Her spirit "spoke" to my spirit.

President Boyd K. Packer taught, "The Holy Ghost speaks with a voice that you feel more than you hear. . . . While we speak of 'listening' to the whisperings of the spirit, most often one describes a spiritual prompting." Further, President Packer cites passages from the Book of Mormon to better explain, "We are told that 'angels speak by the power of the Holy Ghost'. We are even told that when we speak by the power of the Holy Ghost we 'speak with the tongue [or in the same language] of angels' (2 Nephi 31:13; 2 Nephi 32:2)."[16]

I strive daily to pray to my Heavenly Father in the name of Jesus Christ and plead for safety, comfort, and forgiveness. I pledge my complete devotion and obedience to the Father. It is after I recommit that my fears are replaced with courage, my concerns replaced with tranquility, and my downtrodden spirit is filled with hope. The love and respect the Almighty sends through the Holy Ghost is a sure witness of truth. President Joseph Fielding Smith taught, "The Spirit of God speaking to the spirit of man has power to impart truth with greater effect and understanding than the truth can be imparted by personal contact even with heavenly beings."[17]

Because of sincere prayer I can receive personal revelation. I readily notice the ever gentle prodding of the Holy Ghost in answer to my honest communication with the Divine. I recognize these familiar promptings as those I knew in the spirit world. Countless times I have been prompted to simply stop "doing" and "be still." It is during these times of stillness I can identify the power of the Holy Ghost as His spirit communes with mine, resulting in a renewed strength of the Lord's will. These thoughts are communicated in a few seconds but are piercingly clear. It is when I heed these whisperings of the Spirit that I receive aid in calming my worries and, at the same time, increasing my hopes

"For behold, again I say unto you that if ye will enter in by the way, and receive the Holy Ghost, it will show unto you all things what ye should do" (2 Nephi 21:5). "But the Comforter, which is the Holy Ghost, whom the Father will send in my name, he shall teach you all things, and bring all things to your remembrance, whatsoever I have said unto you" (John 14:26). Personal revelation seems natural and familiar to the time spent in the spirit world. I feel grateful to my Heavenly Father for this pure, direct, and individual communication.

Along with the blessings of a greater respect for mortality, knowledge of sincere prayer and personal revelation, I have also been blessed with knowing the empathy and concern my loved ones living on the other side, have for me. Realizing this truth not only intensifies my love for them but also causes me to be more conscious of them. I can more fully comprehend the complex reality of life after death and the association with the spirit world. Such is inherently simple. I have gained an enduring connection to the next life. Likewise, I now have an ongoing and expanding appreciation of those living beyond the veil who sincerely assist and guide me as I struggle through mortality. Heavenly assistants urge my spirit to obey and persevere. This awareness is much more than simply feeling the presence of spirits or personages: it is a certain knowledge that loved relatives and friends who have died indeed live, though I cannot see them. The Holy Ghost strongly testifies of the surety of the spirit world.

Combined, these three concepts have heightened my level of trust, strengthened my faith, and increased my testimony of Jesus Christ.

NOTES

1. Ring, *Heading Toward Omega*, 23.
2. Top, *Glimpses Beyond Death's Door*, 249.
3. Moody, *The Light Beyond*, 38.
4. Ring, 20.
5. Moody, *The Light Beyond*, 40.
6. Ibid., 15; Crowther, *Life Everlasting*, 213.
7. Moody, *Life after Death*, 69.
8. Ibid., 131
9. Ibid., 159.

10. Ibid., 184.
11. Ritchie, *Ordered to Return,* 15.
12. Neal, *To Heaven and Back,* xii.
13. Moody, *The Light Beyond,* 85.
14. Alexander, *Proof of Heaven,* 200.
15. Neal, 219.
16. Packer, "The Gift of the Holy Ghost," 59–62.
17. Smith, "The Sin against the Holy Ghost," 431.

Chapter 13
LEARNING IN THE SPIRIT WORLD

As you probably suspect, NDEers routinely report that learning in the spirit world is exponentially easier and faster, and you don't forget anything. (I can't fathom existence without constantly searching for my wallet and car keys.) And it gets even better; you will have all the knowledge you attained in mortality that "escaped" your mortal brain. Although your brain has forgotten many things, your mind has not. Every event of your life and all that you have learned and experienced lives on in the mind, and is regained after mortality.[1] You will not only recollect every event, but you will also remember the associated emotions and feelings. You will be aware of how your words and deeds affected others. Dr. Neal said of her life review, "I was shown events in my life, not in isolation but in the context of their unseen ripple effects . . . to see the impact of events or words dozens of times removed was profoundly powerful. . . . I was able to clearly see that every action, every decision, and every human interaction impacts the bigger world in far more significant ways than we could ever be capable of appreciating."[2]

The NDE researcher Dr. Moody quoted an NDEer who recounted his life review: "It showed me not only what I had done but even how what I had done had affected other people. . . . I found out that not even your thoughts are lost. . . . Every thought was there. . . . When I got back from this I was very repentant."[3]

Thirst for Knowledge

The desire to attain knowledge is apparently stronger postmortally. This may be related to the desire to progress to a higher realm. Said Joseph Smith, "A man is saved no faster than he gains knowledge."[4]

One NDEer, as quoted by Duane Crowther, expressed it as "a burning thirst for knowledge."[5]

Highly educated Monsignor Benson explained, "The pursuit of knowledge is far greater here than upon the earth-plane, since the necessity of turning our minds to the pressing need and exigencies of incarnate life no longer exist here."[6]

Benson also instructed us that the realm assignment in the spirit world is not contingent alone upon the knowledge one acquires in mortality. To me this reflects the justice of a loving God. Some have mental handicaps or learning disabilities. One of our daughters has a severe mental handicap that prevents her from comprehending above the three- or four-year-old level. Others lived, or now live, with little exposure to knowledge, lacking even the opportunity for basic literacy. Others' circumstances may have demanded, or even now demand, full-time attention to the essentials of existence. God's plan includes mercy and opportunity for all mankind.

All Knowledge

Trying to stay abreast of the Information Age, it's difficult for me to even visualize the far superior spirit world educational systems. When I was young, our telephone was a party line; about eight families shared one line. Television started its broadcast day at 3:00 p.m. and signed off at 11:00 p.m. For several years we received only one station. And here I am, falling further behind in the Information Age, yet attempting to describe a far more advanced system.

In his research, Dr. Moody reported that some NDEers experience a "vision of knowledge." Stated one whom he interviewed, "It seemed that all of a sudden, all knowledge—of all that had started from the very beginning, that would go on without end—that for a second I knew all the secrets of all ages, all the meaning of the universe, the stars, the moon—of everything. . . . It was in all forms of communication, sights, sounds, thoughts. It was any—and everything. It was as if there was nothing that wasn't known. All knowledge was there, not just one field, but everything."[7]

Eadie believes that she had one-on-one "tutoring" by the Savior Himself:

> His light now began to fill my mind, and my questions were answered even before I fully asked them. His light was knowledge. . . . The answers were absolute and complete. . . . Things were coming back to me from long before my life on earth. . . . I could understand volumes in an instant. It was as if I could look at a book and comprehend it at a glance—as though I could just sit back while the book revealed itself to me in every detail, forward and backward, inside and out, every nuance and possible suggestion, all in an instant. As I comprehended one thing, more questions and answers would come to me, all building on each other, and interacting as if all truth were intrinsically connected. The word "omniscient" had never been more meaningful to me.[8]

Obviously, these two had only a glimpse of the environment where all knowledge exists. They did not receive and retain all knowledge; they were merely momentarily exposed to it. Were it not so, what a huge advantage they would possess when returning to mortality.

Assisted Learning

From her NDE, Dr. Neal learned that gaining knowledge in the spirit world is facilitated because there is 'life," or "animation," in everything, and that life "shares" knowledge.[9]

Crowther quoted one NDEer as saying, "We're able to absorb knowledge by holding or touching, seeing, [or] being close to something."[10]

Continuing Learning

Let's not forget that the majority of NDErs have visited only one realm. Monsignor Benson visited seven. Said he of knowledge and learning, "There are many, many things here that we do not understand—and it will take eons of time before we even have a faint gleam of understanding them."[11]

We will take a broader look at knowledge and learning in chapter 17, where we compare our mortal brain to our eternal mind.

Teachers

There are superb teachers available in the spirit world. (We will learn about the very special spirit world teachers of children in chapter 16.)

Although teachers are mentioned in several of my sources, only Benson has given us details on their service:

> Edwin [his guide] pointed out to us the dwelling places of many of the teachers in the various halls of learning, who preferred to live close to the seats of their work. . . . Edwin said that we should always be welcome should we ever wish to call on any of the teachers. The exclusiveness which must necessarily surround such people when they are incarnate vanishes when they come into the spirit. All values become drastically altered in such matters. The teachers themselves do not cease their own studies because they are teaching. They are ever investigating and learning, and passing on to their pupils what they have thus gained. Some have progressed to a higher realm, but they still retain their interest in their former sphere, and continuously visit it—and their many friends—to pursue their teaching.[12]

Teachers must be proficient in both the conceptual and the practical. There are needs or necessary skills in the spirit world that require both instruction and practice to become proficient.[13] Examples include traveling at high speed and to different times. To explain these is beyond the scope of this study; we will learn soon enough, and until we make that transition, we have no need to know.

Libraries

Several NDEers mentioned the great libraries in the spirit world. In fact, there are entire cities dedicated to diverse learning centers. Benson calls them "temples" in which spirit people learn about innumerable subjects, yet each accenting consciousness "of the eternal thanks that we owe to the Great Father."[14] Because the books have their own "life," they "respond" to the inquirer.

Dr. Moody, from his research, learned that in the spirit world should someone focus on any particular thing, knowledge would "flow" from that object to the inquirer.[15] A non-reader could apparently be "tutored" by the book itself, through his or her thoughts (perhaps similar to how the Holy Spirit communicates to mortals).

In these learning centers, or libraries, there can be no falsehood or prejudicial information. Benson provided a particular example regarding political history (one of my favorite studies). He visited an "apartment" that contained the histories of all the nations upon the earth-plane. Said he:

> To anyone who has a knowledge of earthly history, the volumes with which the shelves in this section of the great library were filled, would prove illuminating. The reader would be able to gain, for the first time, the truth about the history of his country. Every word contained in these books was the literal truth. Concealment is impossible, because nothing but the truth can enter these realms.
>
> I have since returned to this library and spent much profitable time among its countless books. I have particularly dipped into history, and I was amazed when I started to read. I naturally expected to find that history would be treated in the manner with which we are familiar, but with the essential difference that now I should be presented with the truth of all historical acts and events. The latter I soon discovered to be the case, but I made another discovery that for the first moment left me astounded. I found that side by side with the statements of pure fact of every act by persons of historical note, by statesmen in whose hands was the government of their countries, by kings who were at the head of those same countries, side by side with such statements was the blunt naked truth of each and every motive governing or underlying their numerous acts—the truth beyond disputation. Many such motives were elevated, many, many of them were utterly base; many were misconstrued, many distorted. Written indelibly on these spirit annals were the true narratives of thousands upon thousands of human beings, who, whilst upon their earthly journey, had been active participants in the affairs of their country. Some were victims to others' treachery and baseness; some were the cause or origin of such treachery and baseness. None was spared, none omitted. It was all there for all to see—the truth with nothing extenuated, nothing suppressed. These records had no respect of persons, whether it be king or commoner, churchman or layman. The writers had just laid down the veridical story as it was. It required no adornment, no commentary. It spoke for itself. And I was profoundly thankful for one thing—that this truth had been kept from us until such time as we stood where we were now standing, when our minds would, in some measure, be prepared for revelations such as were here at hand.[16]

Monsignor Benson mentioned the option of actually reading books, as opposed to receiving the knowledge in the other available ways. In the same vein, Crowther related an NDE that suggests that in the spirit world one often reads conventionally when doing so for pleasure.[17] Apparently, we will still be able to relax, snuggle up, and get lost in a good book.

Multimedia

NDEers reference many means of communication: speaking the many languages of the earth, mental telepathy (which sometimes includes understanding a person's intents and feelings), receiving knowledge just from pondering an issue, totally comprehending an object just from touching it, seeing in vision what another person is describing (similar to Moroni's description of the Hill Cumorah appearing in Joseph's mind), even speaking a pure language in which a person can express perfectly his or her intent or message, with no possibility for misunderstanding. Swedenborg declared that this "pure" language was spoken only in the highest realm.[18] (Could this be the Adamic language?)

Some Final Points

Some NDEers have stated that light and knowledge are synonymous,[19] that knowledge plus experience equals intelligence,[20] and that learning by experience is faster in mortality than in the spirit realms.[21] This last observation reminds me of a Mark Twain axiom: "A man who carries a cat by the tail learns something he can learn in no other way."[22]

Rachel's Experience

While visiting the spirit world I had the ability to learn and communicate perfectly through the Holy Ghost. The clarity of knowledge was immense, the acquisition eternal. Though this explanation may sound quite overwhelming, it was truly the opposite. All information seemed simple and non-threatening to learn. I experienced this sacred process of gaining and exchanging information with far more certainty than I had ever thought possible. Gram and I spoke nonverbally, yet our discussions were completely clear. The experience far exceeded mind-reading trickery, rather approached the understanding that comes with the testifying power of the Holy Ghost. My understanding of her was so utterly clear, so precise, that we quickly agreed on how to resolve my circumstances. I had never before experienced the ease of understanding another with such exactness. I was not only vividly aware of her thoughts but also her views and opinions. Interestingly, it wasn't necessary for her to speak out loud, but I did need her consent to discover what she wished to share.

NOTES

1. Crowther, *Life Everlasting,* 215; Nelson, *Beyond the Veil,* 43.
2. Neal, *To Heaven and Back,* 57.
3. Moody, *Reflections on Life after Death,* 168–69.
4. Smith, *Teachings of the Prophet Joseph Smith,* 217.
5. Crowther, 213.
6. Borgia, *Life in the World Unseen,* 48.
7. Moody, 148–49.
8. Eadie, *Embraced by the Light,* 44–45.
9. Neal, 102.
10. Crowther, 216.
11. Borgia, 33.
12. Borgia, 71.
13. Crowther, 202.
14. Borgia, 51.
15. Moody, 151.
16. Borgia, 46–47.
17. Crowther, 221.
18. Top ,*Glimpses Beyond Death's Door,* 64.
19. Crowther, 217.
20. Ibid., 213.
21. Ibid., 226.
22. See brainyquote.com/quotes/mark_twain_105031.

Chapter 14
SOCIALITY IN THE SPIRIT WORLD

Joseph Smith taught that the same sociality exists there as it does here (see D&C 130:2). I appreciate President Oaks' clarification that "this may describe a kingdom of glory rather than the spirit world, since it continues, 'Only it will be coupled with eternal glory, which glory we do not now enjoy.'"[1]

Casting Your Bread upon the Waters

We will be starkly aware of how our sociality in mortality had far-reaching effects. Eadie recorded, "I saw the disappointment that I had caused others, and I cringed as their feelings of disappointment filled me, compounded by my own guilt. I understood all the suffering I had caused, and I felt it. I began to tremble. I saw how much grief my bad temper had caused, and I suffered this grief. I saw my selfishness, and my heart cried for relief. How had I been so uncaring?"[2] She also referred to the aforementioned ripple effect: "I saw how I had often wronged people and how they had turned to others and committed a similar wrong. The chain continued from victim to victim, like a circle of dominoes, until it came back to the start—to me, the offender. . . . I had offended far more people than I knew, and my pain multiplied and became unbearable."[3]

Now that Sister Eadie's experience has sent us on a guilt trip, let's try to soften it. At her time of greatest remorse, Sister Eadie received comfort:

"Then I felt the love of the [spirit world] council come over me. They watched my life with understanding and mercy. Everything about me was taken into consideration, how I was raised, the things I had been taught, the pain given to me by others, the opportunities I had received or not received."[4]

Stated Benson: "So many of us here in the spirit world are surprised when we discover that some small service that we have done—and immediately afterwards forgotten—has helped us in our spiritual progression to an extent that we should scarcely thought possible."[5]

C. S. Lewis expressed eloquently the eternal significance of our relationship with others: "It's a serious thing to live in a society of possible gods and goddesses, to remember that the dullest and most uninteresting you talk to may one day be a creature which, if you saw it now, you would be strongly tempted to worship, or else a horror and a corruption such as you now meet, if at all, only in a nightmare. All day long we are, in some degree, helping each other to one or another of these destinations."[6]

President James E. Faust taught, "I believe the kind and merciful God, whose children we are, will judge us as lightly as He can for the wrongs we have done and give us the maximum blessings for the good we do."[7]

Stated Elder Orson Pratt: "[There are those who] have never desired to injure any of the children of men, male or female. What do these reflections produce? They produce joy, satisfaction, peace, consolation, and this joy is a hundred fold more intense than what the spirit is capable of perceiving or enjoying in this life. . . . Our spirits then will be happy, far more happy than what we are capable even of conceiving, or having the least idea of in this world."[8]

"The Preacher" said it well, "Cast thy bread upon the waters: for thou shalt find it after many days" (Ecclesiastes 11:1).

Spirit World Occupations

Benson declared, "This is no land of 'eternal rest.' There is rest in abundance for those who need it. But when the rest has restored them to full vigor and health, the urge to perform some sensible, useful task rises up within them, and opportunities abound."[9]

We have made reference of some of the occupations available in the spirit world, but we have yet to mention one of the primary—ongoing construction. Necessitated by a constant influx of transitioning souls and, therefore, a constant need of more housing, parks, gardens, libraries, and so on, the sheer magnitude of spirit world construction calls for deeper examination.

Benson details the addition of a new wing to the same library that we visited in chapter 10:

> As soon as some new [public] building [or addition] is desired, the ruler of the realm is consulted. . . . The ruler then transmits the request to those in authority above him, who in turn refer it to those still higher. We then foregather in the central temple in the city where we were received by one whose word is law, the great soul who, many years ago of earthly time, made it possible for me to communicate thus with the earth world.
>
> Now, this seemingly involved procedure of passing on our request from one to another, may suggest to the mind the tortuous methods of officialdom with its delays and protractedness. The method may be somewhat similar, but the time taken in performance is a very different matter. It is no exaggeration to say that within minutes our request has been stated, and the permission—with a gracious blessing accompanying it—has been granted. On such occasions as these we have cause for rejoicing, and we seize the opportunity to the full.
>
> The next step is to consult the architect, and it may be readily imagined that we have a host of masters upon whom we can draw without limitation. They work for the sheer joy it brings them in the creation of some grand edifice to be used in the service of their fellows. These good men collaborate in a way that would be almost impossible in upon the earth-plane. Here they are not circumscribed by professional etiquette, or limited by the narrowness of petty jealousies. Each is more than happy and proud to serve with the other, and never is there discord or disagreement through endeavoring to introduce, or force, the individual ideas of the one at the expense of another's. Perhaps you will say that such complete unanimity is far and away beyond the bounds of human nature and that such people would not be human if they did not disagree, or otherwise show their individuality.
>
> Before you dismiss my statement as highly improbable, or all the painting of a picture of perfection impossible to attain except in the highest realms of all, let me state the simple fact that discord and disagreement, upon such a matter as we are now considering, could not possibly exist in this realm wherein is my home. And if you still insist that this is impossible, I say No—it is perfectly natural. Whatever gifts we may possess in spirit, it is part of the essence of this realm that we

have no inflated ideas of the power or excellence of those gifts. We acknowledge them in humility alone, without self-importance, unobtrusively, selflessly, and we are grateful for the opportunity of working, con amore, with our colleagues in the service of the Great Inspirer. . . . After the plans for the new buildings [or wings] have been drawn up in consultation with the ruler of the realm, there is a meeting of the master-masons. The latter were mostly masons when they were upon the earth-plane, and they continue to exercise their skill in spirit lands. They do so, of course, because the work appeals to them, even as it did when they were incarnate, and here they have faultless under which they can carry on their work. They do so with a grand freedom and liberty of action that was denied them upon earth, but which is their heritage here in the spirit world. Others, who were not masons by trade, have since learned the spirit methods of building—for the sheer joy of doing so, and they give valuable aid to their more skilled confreres.

The masons, and one other, are the only people concerned in the actual construction, since spirit buildings do not require much that has to be included within the disposition of earthly buildings. Such, for example, as the necessary provision for lighting by artificial means, and for heating. Our light comes from the great central source of all light, and the warmth is one of the spiritual features of the realm.

The addition which was being made to the library consisted of an annex [and] was not, therefore, what one would denominate a major effort, and it required the help of but a comparative few. It was simple in design, consisting of two or three medium-sized rooms.

We were standing fairly close to the group of architects and masons, headed by the ruler of the realm. I noticed particularly that they had all the appearance of being extremely happy and jovial, and many were the jokes that circulated round this cheerful band.

It was strange . . . to think that a building was shortly to go up, because since my arrival in the spirit world I had seen no signs of any building operations going on anywhere . . . At length there were signs that a beginning was to be made. It must be remembered that the act of building in the spirit world is essentially an operation of thought. It will not be surprising, therefore, when I tell you that nowhere were there to be seen the usual materials and paraphernalia associated with earthly builders, the scaffolding and bricks and cement, and the various other familiar objects. We were to witness, in fact, an act of creation—of creation by thought—and as such no "physical" equipment is necessary.

The ruler of the realm stepped forward a few paces, and, with his back toward us, but facing the site upon which the new wing was to arise, he spoke a brief but appropriate prayer. In simple language he asked the Great Creator for His help in the work they were about to undertake.

His prayer brought an immediate response, which was in the form of a bright beam of light that descended upon him. As soon as this happened the architects and masons moved up close beside him.

All eyes were now turned upon that vacant spot beside the main building, to which we noticed that a second beam of light was passing directly from the ruler and the masons. As the second beam reached the site of the annex, it formed itself into a carpet of coruscation upon the ground. This gradually grew in depth, width, and height, but it seemed, as yet, to lack any suggestion of substance. It matched the main building in color, but that was all so far.

Slowly the form gained in size until it reached the required height. We could now see plainly that it matched the original structure in general outline, while the carved devices similarly corresponded.

While it was in this state the architects approached and examined it closely. We could observe them moving within it, until at length they passed from view. They were gone but a moment when they returned to the ruler with the report that all was in order . . . this rather ghostly edifice was in reality an adumbration of the finished structure, shaped in exact facsimile before an intensification of thought was applied to produce a solid and completed building. Any mistake or fault would be detected when the building was in this tenuous state, and corrected at once.

No rectification, however, being necessary in this particular instance, the work was proceeded with immediately."

The downstream of light now became very much more intense, while the horizontal stream from the ruler and his collaborators assumed, after the lapse of a minute or two, a small degree of intensity. We could now perceive the nebulous form acquiring an unmistakable appearance of solidarity as the concentration of united thought laid layer upon layer of increased density upon the simulacrum.

From what I observed it seemed to devolve upon the ruler to supply to each of just that quantity and description of force that each required upon his separate task. He acted, in fact, as distributive agent for the magnetic power [remember the 'snow' principle] that was descending directly upon him. This split up into a number of individual shafts of light of different color and strength, which corresponded with his direct appeals to the Great Architect. There was no faltering or diminution of the application of thought substance to be perceived anywhere.

> The masons themselves seemed to work with a complete unanimity of concentration, since the building attained full solidarity with a remarkable degree of evenness.
>
> After what to appeared [to be] a very short period, the building ceased to acquire any further density, the vertical and horizontal rays were cut off, and there stood before us the finished wing, perfect in every detail, an exact match and extension to the main edifice, beautiful alike in color and form, and worthy of the high purpose to which it was to be devoted.
>
> We moved forward to examine more closely the results of the feat that had just been accomplished. We ran our hands over the smooth surface, as though to convince ourselves that it was really solid![10]

Monsignor Benson now provides an example of transitioning from the various earthly occupations to spirit world professions: "It might be said that with most of us on the earth-plane have had a two-fold existence—our home life and the life connected with our business or occupation. In the latter we associate, perhaps, with an entirely different group of people. It is therefore in the natural order of things, here in the spirit, that much the same state of things should also exist. The scientist, for example, will meet, first of all, his own family connections. When the question of work is broached he will find himself among his old colleagues who have passed into the spirit world before him, and he will again feel more at home. And he will be more than overjoyed at the prospect of the scientific research that stretches before him."[11]

Remember, Monsignor Benson inhabits a middle realm. It appears that those in the highest realm(s) are heavily engaged in the plan of salvation. President Wilford Woodruff stated that the martyred Prophet Joseph Smith frequently visited him: "Joseph Smith continued visiting myself. . . . He said he could not stop to talk to me because he was in a hurry. . . . I saw the prophet again. Now, said I, I want to know why you are in a hurry. I have been in a hurry all of my life, but I expected my hurry would be over when I got into the kingdom of heaven, if I ever did.

"Joseph replied, 'Every dispensation . . . has a certain amount of work to do. . . . Each dispensation has had ample time. . . . We have not. We are the last dispensation, and so much work has to be done, and we need to be in a hurry in order to accomplish it.'"[12] Apparently, in at least paradise, the hurried nature of the last dispensation continues but without hassle or fatigue. Further, it would be in the nature of the inhabitants of paradise to "be anxiously engaged in a good cause [doing] many things of their own free will, and [bringing] about much righteousness" (D&C 58:27) and hurrying to do so.

Spirit World Animals

Animals play a big part in most people's lives. Do these creatures go on to live in the spirit world? In Doctrine and Covenants 77, the Prophet Joseph Smith explained portions of the Revelation of St. John. He said that in paradise, "the spirit of the beast and every other creature which God has created" (vs. 3).

Young Colton Burpo noted seeing "animals of every kind."[13] Later in the same book he was more specific, mentioning "Jesus' horse . . . dogs . . . birds, even a lion—and the lion was friendly, not fierce."[14]

Many NDEers speak of traveling through a tunnel in passage to the spirit world. Eadie said of her experience in the tunnel, "I became aware of other people as well as animals traveling with me."[15] Summarizing several NDEs, Brent Top stated, "Cattle, horses, sheep, and lions are mentioned."[16]

Sarah Menet noted the lack of insects in the realm she visited: "I did not see any insects in the spirit world. It was my understanding that when they cross over they go to an entirely different place prepared just for them—a lower world, sort of a spirit world for insects."[17]

Husbands and Wives

What about spouses, the ultimate and most intimate of socialities? I found several accounts of greeting one's deceased spouse during the NDE. Benson, the only person cited in this work who remains in the spirit world, was a priest while in mortality and therefore did not marry. He mentioned spouses only once in his first book: "All the while our host was explaining these matters. . . . Edwin was busily engaged in conversation with our host's wife."[18]

However, in his third book he taught, "There are many couples to be found living here; for example, a husband and wife who were happily married upon the earth, admirably suited to each other, and with a real bond of affection between them."[19]

What if two who were spouses in morality qualify for different spirit world realms? Benson provided a case in point: "The wife passes into the spirit world and attains to a certain sphere. Later on the husband in turn passes into spirit life, but goes to occupy a realm lower than that of his wife. But the mutual affection still exists, and so the wife takes up her life in the lower sphere in order to be with her husband and help him in his progression."[20]

Monsignor Benson qualified his observations frequently, clarifying that they come exclusively from the parts of the spirit world with which he is acquainted.[21] It appears that the eternal sanctity of marriage and the potential for eternal posterity is reserved for higher realms, or more probable, for after the Resurrection.

Shortly after the American Civil War (1861–65), Rebecca Ruter Springer experienced an NDE, and one that she supposed to be the Savior reasoned with her concerning eternal marriage. Her NDE was apparently long in spirit world "time," and she was missing her "dear husband":

> Suddenly a soft touch rested upon my bowed head, and a Voice I had learned to recognize and love beyond all things in earth or heaven said: "Have I not said truly, though he were dead, yet shall he live again? [Apparently quoting John 11:25–6. The Savior, or messenger, seems now to be speaking in general terms that could apply to any married couple]. What are now the years of separations, since the meeting again is at hand? Come, and let us reason a little together" the Master said, smiling down into my uplifted face. He took my extended hand into his own, and sitting down beside me continued: "Let us consider what these years have done for you. Do you not feel that you are infinitely better prepared to confer happiness than when you parted from him you love?" [Probably referring to all the things she has learned during her NDE.]
>
> I nodded in glad affirmation. "Do you not realize that you stand upon a higher plane, with more exalted ideas of life and its duties; and that, in the strength of the Father, you two hence forward will walk upward together?"
>
> Again, I gladly acquiesced.
>
> "Is the life here less attractive than it was in the earth life?"
>
> "No, no! A thousand times no" I cried.
>
> "Then there is nothing but joy in the reunion at hand?"
>
> "'Nothing but joy" I echoed. Then the Savior led me on to talk of the one [apparently referring to the pending post-NDE reunion with her husband] so soon to come, and I opened my glad heart to him and told him of the noble life, the unselfish toil, the high aspirations, the unfaltering trust of him I loved. I spoke of his fortitude in misfortune,

his courage in the face of sore trial and disappointment, his forgiveness of even malicious injury; and concluded by saying, "He lived the Christianity many others professed. He always distanced me in that."

The face of the Master glowed in sympathy as I talked, and when I had ceased he said "I perceive that you have discovered the secret which makes marriage as eternal as the years of heaven."

"Oh," I said, "to me, marriage must be eternal! How could it be otherwise when two grow together and become as one? Death cannot separate them without destroying; they are no longer two perfect beings, but one in soul and spirit forever."

"Aye," he answered; "but having the marriage rite pronounced does not produce the change. It is the divinity of soul wedded to soul alone that can do that."

So he lead me on until my soul flew upward as a lark in the early morning. He unfolded to me of the soul life that filled my heart with rapture, but which I may not here reveal.[22]

Although Benson mentioned but little about eternal family relationships, he said that "upon earth the number of generations of a family is fairly limited, but in the spirit world all previous generations of a family are co-existing."[23] He also noted that when he passed through the veil, "there were . . . numbers of friends who were waiting to meet me again after our long separation."[24]

The Fairer Sex

When considering the perception that women seem to get fewer "column inches" of attention in sacred literature [and correspondingly in reports from the spirit world], Elder Maxwell mused about the possible reasons:

> When the real history of mankind is fully disclosed, will it feature the echoes of gunfire or the shaping sound of lullabies? The great armistices made by military men or the peacemaking of women in homes and neighborhoods? Will what happened in cradles and kitchens prove to be more controlling than what happened in congresses? When the surf of the centuries has made the great pyramids so much sand, the everlasting family will still be standing, because it is a celestial institution, formed outside telestial time. The women of God know this. . . . Finally, remember, when we return to our real home, it will be with the "mutual approbation of those who reign in the royal courts on high." There we will find beauty such as mortal eye hath not seen; we will hear sounds of surpassing music which mortal ears hath not heard.

> Could such a regal homecoming be possible without the anticipatory arrangements of Heavenly Mother?[25]

Eternal sociality is one of the primary aspects of the plan of salvation. In the Book of Mormon, Jacob teaches us that "men are that they might have joy" (2 Nephi 2:25). Man can experience full joy only when in the presence of those dearest to him.

When the resurrected Savior visited the land Bountiful, he blessed the people, brought the children close around him, prayed to his father, and, "so great was the joy of the multitude that they were overcome" (3 Nephi 17:18). It was then that he expressed, "my joy is full" (ibid., vs. 20).

Lehi exemplified this in a dream. Speaking of the tree of life, he said, "And it came to pass that I did go forth and partake of the fruit thereof; and I beheld that it was the most sweet, above all that I had ever before tasted. Yea, and I beheld that the fruit thereof was white, to exceed all the whiteness that I had ever seen" (1 Nephi 8:11). Then comes the most telling portion: "And as I partook of the fruit thereof it filled my soul with exceedingly great joy; wherefore, I began to be desirous that my family should partake of it also" (ibid., vs. 12; italics added).

Elder Holland recently expressed that an eternal mansion "could be no more to me than a decaying shack if my beloved Pat and our children were not with me to share that inheritance" ("A Perfect Brightness of Hope," October 2020 general conference). Joy comes only when shared with those we love. This extends beyond family to many others who are dear to us. Some years ago, in association with a stake conference, Elder Holland was to have lunch with us in our home. We were delighted, but at the same time apprehensive. At that time, our mentally handicapped daughter Debbie was struggling with frequent severe seizures that would throw her into a rage, and she would literally attack anyone within range. (Most of our other children's friends were afraid to come to our home.) What if Debbie attacked Elder Holland?

We relished his visit to our home, and Debbie didn't have a seizure while he was here. However, just as he walked out the door, she complained, and we thought, "Oh-oh, here comes the violence." Instead she clarified, "Not him go."

When someone dear to us passes on, we say within ourselves "Not him or her go," but a loving Father, through His only Begotten Son, has prepared for us a glorious post-mortal reunion, wherewith we might have joy.

NOTES

1. Oaks, "Trust in the Lord."
2. Eadie, *Embraced by the Light,* 112.
3. Ibid., 113.
4. Ibid.
5. Borgia, *Here and Hereafter,* 18.
6. Lewis, *Weight of Glory,* 1.
7. Faust, "Woman, Why Weepest Thou?"
8. *Journal of Discourses*, vol. 2, 239–40.
9. Borgia, *Life in the World Unseen,* 110.
10. Ibid., 115–19.
11. Ibid., 170–1.
12. Maxwell, *The Promise of Discipleship*, 106–7.
13. Burpo, *Heaven is for Real*, 69.
14. Ibid., 152.
15. Eadie, 38.
16. Top, *Glimpses Beyond Death's Door,* 122.
17. Menet, *There Is No Death*, 107.
18. Borgia, *Life in the World Unseen,* 94.
19. Borgia, *Here and Hereafter,* 89.
20. Borgia, *Here and Hereafter,* 90.
21. Borgia, *Here and Hereafter,* 110.
22. Springer, *My Dream of Heaven,* 118–19.
23. Borgia, *Here and Hereafter,* 87.
24. Borgia, *Life in the World Unseen,* 18.
25. Maxwell, "The Women of God."

Chapter 15
MISSIONARY WORK

As a church, we have a strong commitment to missionary work no matter where we find ourselves—even after we leave mortality. Let's look at some of the differences from here to there.

One difference is magnitude. Elder Maxwell spoke of the vastness of the spirit world and noted that demographers estimate that sixty to seventy billion people have lived on this earth thus far.[1] Joseph F. Smith saw in vision that the gospel must be preached to all (see D&C 138:30). To illustrate the magnitude of this task, it equates roughly to 40,000 spirit world inhabitants for every member of the Church living today.

An associate of mine who has experienced several NDEs told me that the missionary "discussions" in the spirit world are generally given in the opposite order of how they are usually presented in mortality. He said that the first instruction concerns the temple and the essential ordinances, while the Restoration is usually taught as one of the last principles.

Of the methodology in the spirit world, Swedenborg taught that "each and every individual can be taught as befits his own intrinsic character and his ability to receive."[2]

Swedenborg offered the example of "people devoted to the Mohammedan religion who lived a moral life in the world, recognizing one Divine Being and recognizing the Lord as the Essential Prophet . . . withdraw from Mohammad, because he cannot help them, they approach the Lord, worship Him, and recognize what is Divine about Him; then they are taught in the Christian religion. . . . Mohammedans are taught by angels who were once involved in that religion and have turned to Christianity; the heathen too are taught by their own angels."[3] Brother and Sister Top, from their research, and Monsignor Benson from his experience, find missionary work to be less proactive in the next life. Said the Tops "It appears that people who die without the gospel do not necessarily hear it preached as soon as they enter the spirit world, but only as they are ready."[4]

Benson explained:

> It must not be thought that we were part of a campaign to convert people, in the religious sense in which the word is used on earth. Far from it. We do not interfere with people's beliefs nor their viewpoints; we only give our services when they are asked for in such matters, or when we see that by giving them, we can affect some useful purpose. Neither do we spend our time walking about evangelizing people, but when the call comes for help then we answer it instantly. But there comes a time when spiritual unrest will make itself felt, and that is the turning point in the life of many a soul who has been confined and restricted by wrong views, whether religious or otherwise. Religion is not responsible for all mistaken ideas![5]

Two aspects of Benson's explanation gladden my heart: It sounds as if there is no tracting in the spirit world, and our deeply held misconceptions, even across a very broad range, will eventually be brought into line with truth.

It may be that missionary work is more proactive and has a greater sense of urgency in this life because (1) we are bound by the constraints of time; (2) we are preparing for the pending Second Coming, and the Lord has informed us that the hour is near at hand; and (3) because the world's moral compass is wavering and permissiveness is rampant, preparing for the Second Coming must accelerate as opposition increases.

NOTES

1. Maxwell, *The Promise of Discipleship,* 105.
2. Top, *Glimpses Beyond Death's Door,* 144.
3. Ibid., 144–45
4. Ibid., 145.
5. Borgia, *Life in the World Unseen,* 77.

Chapter 16
SPIRITS OF CHILDREN

There is evidence that children maintain their child stature in the spirit world. The October 1929 *Improvement Era* included a near-death experience by a Sister Ellen Jensen. While on the other side, she witnessed a group of "hundreds of children" singing under the direction of Eliza R. Snow.

A few days before Emma Hale Smith's death (nearly thirty-five years after Joseph's martyrdom), she told her nurse, Elizabeth Revel, that Joseph had come to her in a vision. Emma reported that he said to her, " 'Come with me, it is time for you to come with me.' I put on my bonnet and my shawl and went with him. I did not think that it was anything unusual. I went with him into a mansion, and he showed me through the different departments of that beautiful mansion."[1]

Elizabeth Revel then narrated, "And one room was a nursery. In that nursery was a babe in the cradle. [Emma] said, 'I know my babe, my Don Carlos that was taken from me.' She sprang forward, caught the child up in her arms, and wept with joy over the child. When Emma recovered herself sufficiently, she turned to Joseph and said, 'Joseph, where are the rest of my children.' He said to her, 'Emma, be patient and you shall have all of your children.' Then she saw standing by his side a personage of light, even the Lord Jesus Christ."[2]

One NDEer, when describing spirit world libraries, mentioned "groups of children [who] came running across the lawn with their teacher."[3]

Dr. Alexander observed "children . . . laughing and playing."[4]

Swedenborg proclaimed that children "are borne into heaven and entrusted to angels of the feminine gender who during their physical life had loved children tenderly and also loved God. Because they had in the world loved all children with a virtually maternal tenderness, they accept these as their own. And the children, from their inborn nature, love them as though they were their own mother. Each woman has as many children as she wants from her spiritual parental affection. . . . Once this stage is completed, they are transferred to another."[5]

Swedenborg also described how these spirit children become adults: "Understanding and wisdom constitute an angel. Just as long as these children do not possess these attributes, they are with angels but are not themselves angels. But once they become understanding and wise, they become angels. Further—which surprised me—they do not look like children, but like adults. For at that point they are no longer of a child-like nature, but of a more a mature, angelic nature. . . . The reason that children look more mature as they become more perfect in understanding and wisdom is that understanding and wisdom are spiritual nourishment itself. . . . Children in heaven do not mature beyond the beginning of young adulthood and remain at that point to eternity."[6]

The dream that Joseph F. Smith had as a teenage missionary serving in Hawaii is well known to members of the Church. He dreamt that he visited the spirit world. There, the Prophet Joseph Smith told him he was late, and young Joseph replied, "Yes, but I am clean." In that same vision, Joseph F. Smith reported that he saw his mother, Mary Fielding Smith, and that "she sat with a child in her lap."[7]

Benson provided more detail of children who have passed on: "What of the souls that pass over as children; indeed, what of those, even, who pass into the spirit world at birth? The answer is that they grow as they would have grown upon the earth-plane. But the children here—of all ages—are given such treatment and care as would never be possible in the earth world. The young child, whose mind is not yet fully formed, is uncontaminated by earthly contacts, and on passing into the spirit world it finds itself in a realm of great beauty, presided over by souls of equal beauty. The children's realm has been called the 'nursery of heaven.'"[8]

Benson explained, "The children's realm is a township in itself, containing everything that great minds, inspired by the greatest Mind, could possibly provide for the welfare, comfort and education, and the pleasure and happiness of its youthful inhabitants."[9]

They abide in "the quaintest little cottages such as one was always inclined to believe only belonged to the pages of children's story books. . . . Great numbers of children live in these tiny dwellings, each being presided over by an older child, who is perfectly capable of attending to any situation that might arise."[10]

He said that those selected to teach these children "all undergo an extensive training course before they are adjudged fit to fill the post of teacher to the children, and to conform with, and uphold, the rigidly high standards of the work."[11]

He described the children as all ages, from "those who had been born dead, to the youth of sixteen or seventeen years of earth time."[12]

He also explained that "the mental and physical growth of the child in the spirit world is much more rapid than in the earth world."[13]

The "ruler" of the realm acts, in a general sense, as if he were their parent, and the children look up to him as a father. They are taught primarily spiritual things, and some parts of the earthly curriculum, with many parts of the latter omitted as superfluous.[14]

A dear friend of mine often says that his assignment of choice after this life would be to work with little children who had been abused in mortality, lavishing them with all the love and attention possible to accelerate their healing. Perhaps he may get his wish.

A Mother's "Sacrifice"

A rather unusual NDE may be of some comfort to those who have lost a child. Shortly after the delivery of her daughter, a new mother was visited by a spirit who took her by her right hand. "When he took hold of my hand, I immediately knew him to be the greatest friend I had. I also knew that I was a very special person to him. The thrill of this touch of hands exceeds anything I have experienced on earth, in life as we know it. Our meeting was 'understood'—'sensed'—not visual. He 'told me' he had come for my child. 'My child?' I asked, scarcely able to contain my joy and happiness over the news that one of my own children would be going back with him! It was, I 'knew' a very high honor to be selected for this. I had the honor of being the mother of a very extra special child, and I was so proud that he had picked my child."[15]

The being told her, "I will return for your child in four days."

Four days later, when she was signing her discharge papers it was apparent that something very consequential had occurred: "The nurse was devastated. She knew Tari was dead and I didn't. 'Oh, God,' she wailed, 'your doctor should have been here by now! I'm not supposed to tell you, but I can't let you go on believing that Tari is alive. She died early this morning.'"[16]

She continued, "In the weeks following, I felt no grief for my own loss, but I felt sorry for my friends and relatives who didn't know where Tari was, and couldn't believe—really believe—that my 'experience' was anything more than a vivid dream. . . . Well, I soon realized that my acceptance back into this world depended upon 'pretending' to forget, and 'pretending' to grieve the loss of my baby. So I did this for everybody else's sake—except my husband, who believed me, and gained some comfort from it, second-hand."[17]

You may wish to return to chapter 6 and review what the Prophet Joseph Smith taught about the death of children.

A Child's NDE

Now let's look at an NDE from the innocent view of a child. You may wish to refer to the bibliography entry for *Heaven Is for Real*. Perhaps you have seen the movie. The three-year-old son of a pastor experiences an NDE and comes back with information contrary to much of his father's ecclesiastical training but largely in harmony with the gospel.

Three-year-old Colton said that "there were many, many children in heaven."[18] One day out of the blue he said to his mother, Sonja, "Mommy, I have two sisters."[19] His mother explained that he had but one sister, Cassie, and that perhaps he was including his cousin. Colton replied, "I have two sisters. You had a baby die in your tummy." When Sonja asked who told him that, he replied, "She did, Mommy. She said she died in your tummy."

Todd, Colton's father, explained that losing that baby was the most painful event of Sonja's life. Although they had told Cassie, they felt Colton was too young. As Colton saw the tears in his mother's eyes, he said, "She's okay, God adopted her."

In conformity with her religious training, Sonja asked Colton, "Don't you mean Jesus adopted her?"

Colton replied, "No, Mommy. His Dad did."[20]

Colton's childlike explanation harmonizes well with what my wife Kay felt when we lost a son in the second trimester. She believes the fetus had a spirit, that the time of pregnancy was his mortality, and that if we are faithful, we shall have both him and his deceased brother, Russell, in our eternal family.

I have thought about Swedenborg's and Benson's explanations of childcare being provided by loving spirits, but with little mention of family. Could this be because their experiences took place in a middle realm? I suppose that in paradise the care of infants is gladly conducted by deceased family members, many of whom have covenant ties to these children. Another possibility is that the township spoken of by Benson was not their home or permanent dwelling any more than a school is the permanent home of the attendees. I also suppose that the "hundreds of children" being taught music by Eliza R. Snow were attending a music class taught by her and that most were not under her permanent care.

Further, Swedenborg and Benson are both male, without the sacred and intimate sentiments of womanhood and motherhood. If a woman were to give a description of a child's spirit world circumstance, I believe we would see a more tender, sensitive, and detailed perspective.

If this chapter had to be reduced to one sentence, it might be, "God and the Savior (and multitudes of special women) love and care for little children on both sides of the veil."

Rachel's Experience

As nothing compares to the revered love between a mother and her child, this relationship is also preserved beyond comparison in the spirit world. This bond is irreplaceable. A child who has passed on to the next life is comforted and loved and in no way suffers but will experience an increased joy and happiness, beyond description, when reunited with his or her own mother.

NOTES

1. *Improvement Era*, Oct. 1929.
2. Smith, *The Revised and Enhanced History of Joseph Smith by His Mother*, 451–52.
3. Crowther, *Life Everlasting*, 219.
4. Alexander, *Proof of Heaven*, 65–66.
5. Top, *Glimpses Beyond Death's Door*, 214.
6. Ibid., 215.
7. Crowther, 183.
8. Borgia, *Life from the World Unseen*, 155–56.
9. Ibid., 161.
10. Ibid., 157–58.

11. Ibid., 159.
12. Ibid.
13. Ibid., 160
14. Ibid.
15. Ring, *Heading Toward Omega*, 77–78.
16. Ibid.
17. Ibid., 80–81
18. Burpo, *Heaven is for Real,* 146.
19. Ibid., 94
20. Ibid., 95.

Chapter 17

HOW THE SPIRIT DIFFERS FROM THE BODY

In chapter 9 we talked of the realms of the spirit world. In that chapter I quoted President Brigham Young's apparent vision or NDE-like experience. As an introduction to this chapter, and for your convenience, I include a portion of that quote:

> I have had to exercise a great deal more faith to desire to live than I ever experienced in my whole life to live. The brightness and glory of the next apartment is inexpressible. . . . [In mortality] when we advance in years we have to be stubbing along and be careful lest we fall. But yonder how different! They move with ease and like lightning. If we want to behold Jerusalem as it was in the days of the Savior; or if we want to see the Garden of Eden as it was when created, there we are, and we see it as it existed spiritually, for it was created spiritually and then temporally, and spiritually it still remains. And when there we may visit any city we please that exists upon its surface. If we wish to understand how they are living here on these western islands, or in China, we are there; in fact, we are like the light of the morning. . . . We have the Father to speak to us, Jesus to speak to us, and angels to speak to us and we shall enjoy the society of the just and the pure who are in the spirit world until the resurrection.[1]

Also based on experience or study, President John Taylor stated, "[Death,] this dark shadow and valley so trifling; [one is] passed from a state of sorrow [and] grief . . . into a state of existence where I can enjoy he fullest extent as far as can be done without a body. . . . I thirst more, I want to sleep no more, I hunger no more, I tire no more, I run, I walk, I labor, . . . nothing like pain or weariness. I am full of life, full of vigor."[2]

Young Colton Burpo declared that he had an encounter with "Pop" (his paternal grandfather) in the spirit world. Colton's father brought out a photo of his father and showed it to Colton. Colton's dad expected him to light up in recognition. Instead, he frowned and shook his head, declaring, "Dad, nobody's old in heaven, and nobody wears glasses."[3]

Later, Colton's father located a photo of Pops when he was twenty-nine years old. When he showed it to Colton, Colton said happily, "How did you get a picture of Pops?"[4]

The "curse" of "eating [our] bread by the sweat of [our] brow," as well as the other debilitating things President Taylor mentioned, will be forever gone, allowing us to give much more attention to the things of the kingdom. Our health will be perfect. We will evolve to our physical prime, with no blemishes.[5]

According to Moody's research, the human spirit has density but not "earthly density."[6] We will have the capacity to pass through earthly obstacles.[7]

Furthermore, gravity will not be a detriment to spirits. It will still be a necessary force for much of the environment, such as rivers and streams. Traveling by foot will be more like floating than walking.[8]

In many realms, our clothing will be partially composed of light (and therefore of truth).[9] In at least the higher realms, travel, which requires so much time and effort on earth, can be instant or slow, as we choose,[10] making the vastness of each spirit realm easily manageable.

The Immortal Mind

Let's turn our attention to the mind, freed from the constraints of the mortal brain.

Dr. Eben Alexander is a highly experienced neurosurgeon. His academic preparation encompassed forty years. Although he had attended church as a youth, he completely bought into academia, depending exclusively on physical evidence for knowledge. When his patients envisioned seeing a deceased loved one who invited the patient to pass on, or perhaps expressed a spiritual reassurance of a life beyond, Dr. Alexander was glad for the comfort provided to the patient but gave no credence to these experiences because of the lack of physical evidence. He explained that "modern neuroscience dictates that the brain gives rise to consciousness—to the mind, to the soul, to the spirit, to whatever you choose to call that invisible, intangible part of us that truly makes us who we are—and I had little doubt that it was correct."[11]

His life was devoid of anything spiritual; that is, until he "died."

His attending physicians, who included dear friends, were baffled by the disease that put Dr. Alexander into a coma, but they were no more confounded than he, who was experiencing an NDE. After his physical recovery Alexander declared, "Everything I had learned in four decades of study and work about the human brain, about the universe, and about what constitutes reality conflicted with what I'd experienced during those seven days in a coma."[12]

He was particularly amazed by how much the marvelous human brain actually bridled the human mind. Our physical eyes, in conjunction with our brain, provide the miracle of vision. However, the mind, when unencumbered by the eyes and brain, can "see" in every direction, all of the time. As marvelous as our ears and brain cooperate to provide hearing, for the unrestricted mind, sound and sight are actually one in the same, in perfect harmony with all of our senses. Dr. Alexander realized that the brain is "a kind of reducing valve or filter, shifting the larger, nonphysical consciousness that we possess in the nonphysical worlds down into a more limited capacity for the duration of our mortal lives."[13]

Benson said, "In the spirit world we have no physical brain to hamper us, and our minds are fully and completely retentive of all knowledge that comes to us,"[14] and, "[in the spirit world] our minds, being then free of a heavy physical brain, are at liberty to exercise their powers to the full."[15]

For Dr. Alexander's unfettered mind, knowledge was omnipresent. "Each time I silently posed [a question], the answer came instantly in an explosion of light, color, love and beauty that blew through me like a crashing wave. What was important about these bursts was that they didn't simply silence my questions by overwhelming them. They answered them, but in a way that bypassed language. Thoughts entered me directly. But it wasn't thought like we experience on earth. It wasn't vague, immaterial, or abstract. These thoughts were solid and immediate—hotter than fire and wetter than water—and as I received them I was able to instantly and effortlessly understand concepts that would have taken me years to fully grasp in my earthly life."[16]

Benson noted, "I discovered that my mind was a veritable storehouse of facts concerning my earthly life. Every act I had performed, and every word that I had uttered, every impression I had reached; every fact that I had read about, and every incident I had witnessed, all these, I found, were indelibly registered in my subconscious mind."[17]

Orson Pratt taught, "Every act of our lives will be fresh upon the memory. . . . It is not the want of capacity in the spirit of man that causes him to forget the knowledge he may have learned yesterday; but it is because of the imperfection of the tabernacle in which the spirit dwells. . . . It is, then, this memory that will produce the suffering and the pains upon that class of spirits whose works have been wicked and abominable in the sight of God."[18] The immortal mind can comprehend volumes of information in an instant.[19] Many NDEers have reported the ability to think more lucidly and rapidly.[20] They also report that it is as if they have additional senses. One Church-member NDEer stated, "We're able to absorb knowledge by holding or simply touching, seeing, being close to something. . . . We in essence absorb knowledge through every part of our bodies."[21]

Another person cited in *Life Everlasting* mirrored Dr. Alexander's observation: "My mind was so quick, and I was able to see in every direction at the same time."[22]

Reported another NDEer, "All you would have to do is show me [a] tape recorder and I would be able to comprehend everything about it, instantly, even if I had never seen one before. My ability to comprehend and learn had been multiplied a thousand times or more. The slow, clunky manner in which I learned on earth had evaporated. I could absorb and comprehend things I had never thought possible."[23]

In this life we miscommunicate frequently, causing misunderstanding and even bad feelings. In the spirit world, some sort of telepathy makes misunderstanding impossible. A spirit world guide explained the difference to a man experiencing an NDE: "For instance, if I told you that I wanted to meet you in the park, you'd want to know what park, where in the park, an exact location. I would use words to describe everything the way I understood them. You might not have the same definition for the words I chose. Therefore, a misunderstanding (sic). But, if I sent a message telepathically to you of the same park, you'd see the exact spot as the park I had chosen."[24] Others have said that when spirits communicate mind to mind, even the associated emotions are shared perfectly. Benson calls these "thought links."[25]

Swedenborg professed that in the highest realm the inhabitants speak in a purer and more beautiful language and that "angels can know a person's whole life from the tone, from a few spoken words."[26] Perhaps this is the Adamic language (see Moses 6:5–6).

Some may feel uncomfortable with the idea of "broadcasting" our thoughts. Swedenborg explained, "Your thoughts are private. If you need to communicate with someone, then you project out to someone, or to a group, or to everyone here. When you are only thinking to yourself, your mind has a way of shutting out or shielding itself from thought leakage."[27]

Anatomy and Physiology of Our Spirits

In his third book, Benson teaches us some spirit world anatomy and physiology. He reiterates the relationship of the mind to the mortal brain: "There are many things that we have to unlearn and re-learn when we first come to dwell in the spirit lands, but our minds, being then free of a heavy physical brain, are at liberty to exercise their powers to the full."[28]

The mind can quickly learn, living in these very different conditions of existence, how to enhance one's capacities by abiding to spiritual laws. For example, for a spirit, mere thoughts are a powerful mode to accomplish something. After sufficient study and practice, a spirit can travel immense distances quickly and accurately. No spirit is ever "lost in the woods." A spirit can create (or perhaps, "organize from matter unorganized" may be a better expression) a building, a city, a research facility, a garden, a library, a temple, or much more just by applying the powerful thought processes that he has studied, practiced, and learned. This process seems to align well with the scriptural accounts of the Creation.

With this great power of thought, we might suppose that our hands are unnecessary. Benson explained why this isn't true:

> Because we can create so much with our minds, because we can fabricate things by the close application of thought, then, it might be imagined that there is precious little left for our hands to do, except to make up our full complement of limbs, and so obviate our presenting ourselves as something of monstrosities. The truth is that we use our hands in a thousand different actions during what you would call the day's work. . . . For example, in our spirit homes we pick up a book, we open or close a door, we shake hands with some friend who calls; we arrange some flowers upon the table; we paint a picture or play upon a musical instrument; or we may operate a scientific apparatus of

> some sort. . . . We like to employ our hands in conjunction with our minds. . . . There are plenty of things that could be created in these realms purely by thought and without the least interposition of hands, but we like to go the long way round sometimes and find some employment for our hands.[29]

He said that it is much the same with our feet: "We like to walk just as we used to upon earth."[30] Spirit beings are capable of walking hundreds of miles with no fatigue, but for great distances they generally "think" themselves there, as previously discussed.

Gravity exists in the spirit world. It is an obvious requirement for buildings, streams, timbers, and the like, but human beings are not subservient to it.[31] This implies that if you want to walk your dog, you can do just that, in a beautiful and comfortable environment.

Monsignor Benson taught that spirits "breathe. . . . The spirit world has air just as you have on earth, and we have lungs in our bodies with which to breathe it. And it does 'oxygenate' the blood in what would be the spirit world equivalent of that process. . . . While your blood undergoes the process of oxygenating, our blood is reinvigorated by the spiritual force and energy that is one of the principal constituents of the air we breathe here."[32]

Unlike mortals, spirits have no requirement for food or drink: "We derive another part of our sustenance from the light of these realms, from the abundance of colour, from the water, from the fruit when we wish to eat of it, from the flowers, and from all that is beautiful itself, . . . but we also take strength from the great spiritual force that is being constantly poured down upon us from the Father of Heaven Himself."[33]

Personally, I suspect that this force is what the scriptures call the Light of Christ.

NOTES

1. *Teachings of the Presidents of the Church—Brigham Young*, 282–23.
2. Maxwell, *The Promise of Discipleship*,106.
3. Burpo, *Heaven Is for Real*, 21.
4. Ibid., 22.
5. Borgia, *Life from the World Unseen*, 152.
6. Moody, *Life after Life*, 48.
7. Ibid., 34; Top, *Glimpses Beyond Death's Door*, 41.
8. Crowther, *Life Everlasting*, 200.
9. Top, 48.

10. Moody, 38.
11. Alexander, *Proof of Heaven*, 59.
12. Ibid., 218.
13. Ibid., 125.
14. Borgia, *Life from the World Unseen,* 130.
15. Borgia, *Here and Hereafter*, 105.
16. Alexander, 76.
17. Borgia, *Life from the World Unseen*, 150.
18. Journal of Discourses, vol. 2, 239–40.
19. Crowther, 44.
20. Moody, 37; Crowther, 213.
21. Crowther, 216.
22. Ibid., 214.
23. Moody, *The Light Beyond*, 45.
24. Crowther, 200; This is much like Moroni's communication to Joseph Smith concerning the location of the plates.
25. Borgia, *Life from the World Unseen*, 180.
26. Top, 67.
27. Ibid.
28. Borgia, *Here and Hereafter*, 105–6.
29. Ibid., 106.
30. Ibid.
31. Ibid., 109.
32. Ibid., 111.
33. Ibid., 111–12.

Chapter 18
FREE FROM FRUSTRATION

We have already discussed many earthly challenges that do not exist in the spirit world, such as disease and tribulation. This chapter enumerates a few of the earthly frustrations that do not exist in at least the middle and higher realms of the spirit world.

Benson stated that there is no hustle, bustle, or hurrying. Time is measured differently, and one has much more control over it. Transportation, after proper study and practice, can be instantaneous.[1] It is impossible to "waste time." "Nobody ever wasted time here, because there is no time to waste."[2] Benson also taught the following:

- There are no recurring seasons.[3]
- In the middle realm where Benson dwells, there is no boredom, loneliness, depression, anxiety, pain, suffering, calamities, accidents, discomfort, illness (mental, physical, nor emotional), fear, fatigue, confinement (except to one's spacious realm), self-consciousness, unhappiness, unpleasantness, discord, discomfort, discontentment; the list could go on and on.[4]
- Many earthly occupations are not required: police officers, lawyers, medical personnel, firemen, psychologists, diplomats, and many others. In fact, my previous profession as a military pilot would fall into this category.
- There are no compass points (north, south, east, west). Destinations are seen in the mind prior to travel, and spirits have the inherent

ability to arrive precisely there [after practice and training] without external references.[5]

- There are no national boundaries. One is free to travel anywhere within the spacious confines of one's realm.[6]
- There is no commerce: no bartering, buying, nor selling. However, there is "earning" and "ownership."[7] Benson expresses it thus: "There is ownership in the spirit world. Indeed, why should there not be? Ownership, however, is gained in a different way from that of the earth. There is only one right of ownership in the spirit world, and that is the spiritual right. None other will suffice; none other even exists. According to our spiritual right, gained by the kind of life we have lived upon earth, and afterwards according to our progression in the spirit world, so can we possess."[8]

He offered his home as an example: "When the day shall dawn upon which my spiritual progression will carry me onward. I shall leave my house. But it will rest entirely with myself whether I leave my old home as it stands for others to occupy and enjoy, or whether I demolish it. It is customary, I am told, to make a gift of it to the ruler of the realm for his disposal to others at his discretion."[9]

Benson further explained: "It's not by any means everyone who owns a house here. Some people don't want to be bothered with one—though bothered is not the exact word to use, as no home, whether large or small, can possibly be a bother in any earthly sense. But there are folk who don't feel the necessity for a house, and so they don't have one. Perfectly simple. To begin with, the sun is always shining in these and other regions, there's no unpleasant wind or cold. It's always the same steady, unvarying genial warmth. . . . So there is nothing from which we need protection as on earth, in the way of the elements. As for privacy, well, there are myriads of spots . . . that will provide all the solitude you are likely to want."[10]

I will insert here that when Monsignor Benson entered his realm, a replica of his earthly cottage had been prepared from him, with several improvements.[11]

One's accustomed clothing had also been prepared.[12] It makes sense that when a spirit is allowed to show him or herself to a mortal, they are dressed in clothes that the visitant recognizes; it could be considered an additional mode of identification. Benson explains that a spirit soon chooses to change to the comfortable, shimmering, animated robes of the spirit world.[13]

Speaking of other earthly possessions not required in the spirit world, Benson explained, "Many people arrive here to find themselves richly and abundantly provided with spirit-world possessions that are far in excess of those which they owned upon the earth. And the contrary is often the case. Possessors of great earthly effects can find themselves spiritually poor when they come here. But they can gain the right to possess more, far more than they ever could own on earth, and of far greater value and beauty."[14]

He added, "In an idle moment you could compile such a list of commodities that are not required for life in the spirit as would reach the dimensions of a store's catalog."[15] Had Benson written this in today's world, "store's catalog" would probably have been replaced by "Amazon" or "eBay."

There are numerous scriptures that speak of heavenly mansions, such as John 14:2, D&C 98:18, Enos 1:27, Ether 12:32, Doctrine and Covenants 59:2, and Doctrine and Covenants 76:111. However, all heavenly ownership (crowns, principalities, and so on) come by individual merit that is 1) made possible by divine grace, 2) relegated to us as we are ready, and 3) on condition that we magnify it. Personal ownership excludes no one from the enjoyment of anything "owned" by anyone else. For example, mansions have no locks and everyone in the realm is welcome to enter. There aren't any "no trespassing" signs. Everyone is welcomed everywhere. The owner ("patron" may be a better word) of an orchard welcomes all to partake of the fruit, yet the fruit is not diminished. It appears that "supply" is infinite, regardless of demand. The law of consecration seems to be lived to its fullest with no poor among them.

This is yet another reminder that our chief correspondent, Monsignor Benson, inhabits a middle realm. I can't personally imagine such unselfish sharing in the lowest realms.

NOTES

1. Borgia, *More About Life from the World Unseen*, 67.
2. Ibid., 141.
3. Borgia, *Life from the World Unseen*, 30.
4. Ibid., 22–23, 115, 145–52.
5. Ibid., 111.

6. Ibid., 126.
7. Borgia, *More About Life from the World Unseen*, 149.
8. Borgia, *Here and Hereafter*, 95.
9. Borgia, *Life from the World Unseen*, 120.
10. Borgia, *More About Life from the World Unseen*, 31.
11. Borgia, *Life from the World Unseen*, 11.
12. Ibid., 10.
13. Ibid., 111.
14. Borgia, *Here and Hereafter*, 55.
15. Borgia, *More About Life from the World Unseen*, 68.

Chapter 19
TRANSITION TO THE SPIRIT WORLD

On July 10, 2018, the Ogden, Utah, *Standard Examiner* newspaper included an article by Gary Rotstein of the *Pittsburg Post-Gazette.* It is entitled "Near Death, Seeing Dead People May be Neither Rare nor Eerie." Rotstein introduces us to Beth Roncevich, who tells of sitting with her mother at the side of the bed of her dying father. Her dying father unexpectedly laughed. She asked what he was laughing at. He said, "Oh, we're all together. Everybody's together and we're having a wonderful time. We're having so much fun."[1]

Roncevich went on to become a hospice nurse. Rotstein subsequently interviewed her and reported that she, and others who work with the dying, speak of patients who have talked about a vision, dream, or hallucination concerning someone who preceded them in death. "It is often a long-lost loved one—mothers are most common, but fathers, siblings, grandparents and even pets also frequently show up, seemingly welcoming to whatever lies next. . . . It is always a calming experience. . . . Even in an unconscious state, their arms will lift up as though taking someone else's hand, and their mouths will move as though speaking to someone."[2]

Rotstein also told of a research study by The Center for Hospice & Palliative Care, located in a suburb of Buffalo, New York. The CEO, Christopher Kerr, stated, "As we approach death, dreams increase dramatically in frequency, and the dreams increasing most frequently have to do with the deceased—the loved ones who have passed."[3]

Kerr said of the study, "Of participants in that study, more than half the time they were reported to be either awake or a combination of asleep and awake during their experiences. In about three-fifths of cases, there was a theme of preparing to go somewhere. In fewer than one of five instances, the patient reported distress from the dream or vision. There's almost like this built-in mechanism of serenity or safety, and the fear of death kind of diminishes. . . . The predominant themes are of love and forgiveness."[4]

Dr. Kerr related that he had advised a nurse that a terminally ill patient still had quality time ahead if given IV antibiotics and other fluids. The nurse suggested otherwise. When Dr. Kerr asked why, the nurse replied, "Because he's seeing his deceased mother."[5]

Rotstein related an experience of Katie Hayes, of the same hospice. "Katie recalled an elderly woman terminally ill with heart disease whom she got to know well over a period of months."[6]

Katie reported, "One day I went to her, and she was in bed. I sat down, and she said, 'Katie, you'll never believe what I saw last night. I saw all of my loved ones who have passed on before me. My mother, husband, sister—they were all standing right at the front of my bed.'

"I said, 'Wow, that is amazing,' and the next day she passed."[7]

Melissa Brestensky, a nurse at a different facility, said, "I've seen patients sit there and have a conversation with someone I couldn't see. I had one particular patient—it was hours later she passed away—she was describing the angels in the hallway, saying, 'Look at how beautiful they are, they are in beautiful white gowns.'"[8]

Darin Martin told of her late husband's sightings before his death: "First, he saw his youngest brother, who had died in 1980, sitting on the couch."[9]

Mrs. Martin said that later her husband made sure that she and his deceased brother stepped out of the way of their deceased Great Dane, Czar.

Martin said, "I truly believe when you die and go to heaven you have family and friends there to meet you."[10]

Maria DePasquale, a hospice nurse for over thirty-eight years, explains how she typically responds to a terminally ill person who reports seeing deceased loved ones and associates: "I maybe ask, 'Well, what do you think they're doing there?' They say something like, 'I think they're telling me it's time, it's time.' Then I say, 'Well, isn't it nice that somebody's there to share that with you.'"[11]

It is very common for NDEers to report meeting and associating with deceased friends and relatives. Some people, as they are beginning to transition to the spirit world, speak of deceased loved ones as if they were present. Many reach out as if being received by someone. Brigham Young, just before his demise, exclaimed "Joseph!" three times.[12]

When I was a young boy, my widowed and elderly maternal grandmother lived with us for several years. She was wonderful, with many godly attributes. I remember threading needles for her as she did our mending. When she was near death, my mother, her sister, and I were with her in her bedroom. Suddenly my mother and aunt turned to each other and said, almost in unison, "Dad is here." I admit that within seconds I was well down the hall, but I soon heard my mother say, "She's gone." I returned to the bedroom and felt the sacred spirit associated with the passing. An initially frightening experience had become my first witness of the reality of the spirit world and of continuing relationships.

Again, we turn to Benson for additional detail:

> To leave the earth world and to take up permanent residence in the spirit world is not such a personal upheaval as some people might be disposed to imagine. . . . When we pass into the spirit world we meet again those of our relatives and friends who have passed over before us. . . . The meetings with relations and friends are something that must be experienced in order to grasp the full significance and joy of reunion. These gatherings will continue for some while after the arrival of the new resident. It is natural that in the novelty both of surroundings and condition some time should be spent in a grand exchange of news, and in hearing of all that has transpired in the spirit lives of those who have "predeceased" us. Eventually the time will come when the newly-arrived individual will begin to consider what he is to do with his spirit life.[13]

To provide you more insights into this transition that awaits all of us, I include a few excerpts from the book *At the Hour of Death* by Karlis Osis and Erlendur Haraldsson, PhDs. A physician reported:

> All of a sudden she opened her eyes. She called her [deceased] husband by name and said she was coming to him. She had the most peaceful, nicest smile just as she were to the arms of someone she

thought a great deal of. She said, "Guy, I am coming." She didn't seem to realize I was there. It was almost as if she were in another world. It was as if something beautiful had opened up to her; she was experiencing something so wonderful and beautiful.[14]

Suddenly she looked eagerly towards one part of the room, a radiant smile illuminating her whole countenance. "Oh, lovely, lovely," she said. I asked, "What is lovely?" "What I see," she said in low, intense tones. "What do you see?" "Lovely brightness—wonderful beings." It is difficult to describe the sense of reality conveyed by her intense absorption in the vision. Then—seeming to focus her attention more intently on one place for a moment—she exclaimed, almost with a kind of joyous cry, "Why, it's Father? Oh, he's so glad I'm coming; he is so glad. It would be perfect if only W. (her husband) would come too."

Her baby was brought for her to see. She looked at it with interest, and then said, "Do you think I ought to stay for baby's sake?" Then turning toward the vision again, she said, "I can't—I can't stay; if you could see what I do, you would know I can't stay."[15]

Deathbed patients see apparitions more often when fully conscious and having proper awareness and capability of responding to the environment than when awareness and communication are impaired.[16]

In a very soft voice, and with a smile on her face, she had an endearing conversation about how much she loved him [her husband], how much she missed him, and how she knew she would join him. She said, "It won't be long now before I'll be with you." Reaching out as if she felt [her husband's] hand, she said "You look well cared for."[17]

"My [dead] grandfather is just near my bed. He has come to take me with him. Please don't leave me alone!" Although the patient's physical condition was serious, his consciousness was quite clear; he was able to respond to questions in a concise, coherent manner. However, the apparition left him scared, with unpleasant emotions. He died within the hour.[18]

Her consciousness was very, very clear—no sedation, no hallucinogenic history. She was cheerful and confident that she would recover and return to her daughter who badly needed her at home. Suddenly she stretched out her arms and, smiling, called to me. "Can't you see Charlie [her dead husband] there with outstretched arms? I'm

> wondering why I haven't gone home before." Describing the vision she said, "What a beautiful place with all the flowers and music. Don't you hear it? Oh, girls, don't you see Charlie?' She said he was waiting for her. I feel she definitely saw her husband."[19]
>
> A Hindu farmer in his fortieth year was suffering from liver disease. He told [his doctor] he felt himself flying through the air and into another world where he saw gods sitting and calling him. He thought he was going to meet those gods; he wanted to be there, saying to those around him, "Let me go." Relatives tried to talk him out of it. He would be O.K. He should not go. But the patient was very happy to see those gods and he was ready to die. He went into a deep coma a short time later, and died in two days. He was clear and coherent while describing what he "saw."[20]
>
> A 68–year-old Polish housewife was afflicted with cancer. Her mind was clear. She was settling some financial matters and asked for her purse. She had not thought of dying. Then she saw her husband who had died twenty years before. She was happy, with a sort of religious feeling, and according to her doctor, she lost all fear of death. Instead of fearing death, she felt it to be the logical, correct thing. She died within 5 or 10 minutes.[21]

These experiences sit well with comments by President James E. Faust in his eighty-third year: "As we get older, the pull from our parents and grandparents on the other side of the veil becomes stronger. It is a sweet experience when they visit us in our dreams."[22] Emma Smith's last words were "Joseph! Yes, yes, I'm coming."[23]

The Other Side of the Veil

The above observations, of course, come from this side of the veil. The "view" from the other side is also noteworthy.

We begin with Benson explaining the "attachment" of the body to the spirit: "The spirit body exactly coincides with the physical body. . . . The former is attached to the latter by a magnetic cord. I call it a magnetic cord for lack of a better name [remember the 'snow' principle]. So long as the magnetic cord is joined to the earthly body, just so long will earthly life remain in the physical body. But the moment that dissolution takes place the life-line is severed, the spirit is free to live in its own element, while the body will decay in the manner which is perfectly familiar to you upon earth."[24]

Benson then explained "normal" separation, "wherein the spirit body becomes gradually and easily detached from the earthly body in a slow and steady process of separation. The magnetic cord, in such cases, will detach from the earthly gently, it will fall away naturally, just as the leaf falls from the tree in the autumn. When the leaf is in full life and vigour (sic) it requires a strong action to dislodge it from the tree. And so it is with the spirit body. In the young the cohesion is firm, but it gradually lessons as age increases."[25]

What about "abnormal" death? Benson provided this example:

> It is when we come to transitions where the physical body is literally disintegrated, blown into fragments in a second of time, that the greatest distress and discomfort are caused to the spirit body. The magnetic cord is snapped off, or wrenched away, almost as though the limb of the physical body were torn from the socket. The spirit body finds itself suddenly dispossessed of its earthly tenement, but not before the physical shock of disintegration has been transmitted to the spirit body. Not only is there extreme bewilderment, but the shock has something of a paralyzing effect. The [spirit] person so situated may be incapable of movement for the time being. In many instances sleep will intervene. He will remain in the place of his dissolution, but we come to his rescue, and carry him away to one of the rest homes specially provided for such cases. Here he will receive treatment from experts, and ultimately the patient will recover his full health beyond any shadow of doubt. The cure is certain and complete. There is no such thing as a relapse or recurrence of the indisposition. Perhaps the most difficult part of the treatment comes when a full consciousness is restored and the patient begins to ask questions![26]

Concerning the nature of the spirit after transition to the spirit world, Benson expressed, "A person is exactly the same the moment after he has 'died' as he was the moment before. No magical, instantaneous change takes place either of mind or body. We pass into the spirit world with all our earthly likes and dislikes, all our fancies and foibles, all our idiosyncrasies, and with all our religious errors fast upon us."[27]

Sound familiar? In the Book of Mormon Amulek expressed it thusly to the Zoramites: "That same spirit which doth possess your bodies at the time that ye go out of this life, that same spirit will have power to possess your body in that eternal world" (Alma 34:34).

Monsignor Benson clarified what he [and Amulek] taught: "We are just as we were on earth, though it does not follow in every instance that we will behave just as we did on earth."[28]

However, the ambiance of the spirit world soon impacts our behavior. Benson explained, "The beauties and charms of these realms act like an intellectual tonic; they bring out only that which is and always was the very best in one. Whatever was not the very best in one upon earth will be swamped by the good nature and kindness which the very air here will bring out, like some choice bloom beneath the warm summer sun. . . . We are no longer subject to the stressed that produce the unpleasant qualities that were observable in us when we were on the earth. Remove the causes of the distempers and the latter will disappear also."[29]

I take this to mean that this change to a much more pleasant environment facilitates improvement for those who desire to improve.

However, because most mortals scarcely ponder our next life, and religious creeds (and our celebrations of Halloween) generally offer a very distorted view of the next world, most of the deceased "arrive in a state of bewilderment and complete ignorance of the fact that they have passed from the earth world."[30]

"The rest for the newly-arrived person is frequently advisable, or necessary," expressed Benson, "to allow of adjustment of the spirit body to its new conditions of life."[31]

Chapter 6 provides details concerning these halls of rest. I believe this "rest" spoken of by Benson is a part of the "rest" promised by the Savior (see Matthew 11:28).

Rachel's Experience

Based on my NDE, I am comforted by the memory of life beyond the grave. I feel tremendously blessed to have discovered the unconditional love of my deceased ancestors.

When my earthly time is complete and it is time to enter the spirit world, which is the next phase of the Lord's plan, I know I will not fear. Although my mortal mind no longer recalls the intricacy of the next life nor understands the vastness of eternity, I know my spirit did. I may feel uncertain up until the precise time of transition, yet I have faith I will remember and comprehend with exactness the details of eternal life, as I have before. I will at last be able to see the faces of my beloved heavenly friends and relatives, and any fear will be replaced with complete peace.

NOTES

1. Rotstein, "Near Death, Seeing Dead People May be Neither Rare nor Eerie."
2. Ibid.
3. Ibid.
4. Ibid.
5. Ibid.
6. Ibid.
7. Ibid.
8. Ibid.
9. Ibid.
10. Ibid.
11. Ibid.
12. Ibid.
13. Borgia, *Life from the World Unseen*, 170.
14. Osis and Haraldsson, *At the Hour of Death*, 4.
15. Ibid., 16–17.
16. Ibid., 32.
17. Ibid., 42.
18. Ibid., 71–72.
19. Ibid., 83.
20. Ibid., 105.
21. Ibid., 113.
22. Faust, "Dear Are the Sheep That Have Wandered."
23. *Encyclopedia of Latter-day Saint History,* 1113.
24. Borgia, *Here and Hereafter,* 15–16.
25. Ibid., 47.
26. Ibid., 48.
27. Ibid., 39.
28. Ibid., 39.
29. Ibid., 124–25.
30. Ibid., 21.
31. Ibid., 45.

Chapter 20
LIGHT AND LOVE

If this book had to be condensed into just a few words, I would choose the Light of God and the Love of God. It seems appropriate, in the last chapter of our study and of our worship, to share some efforts of NDErs to describe this light and love:

> It was a total immersion in light, brightness, warmth, peace, security.[1]

> There was the warmest, most wonderful love. Love all around me . . . I felt light-good-happy-joy-at ease. Forever—eternal love.[2]

> The light communicates to you and for the first time in your life . . . is a feeling of true, pure love. It can't be compared to the love of your wife, the love of your children. . . . All of these wonderful, wonderful feelings combined could not possibly compare to the feeling, the true love.[3]

> Love is, without a doubt, the basis of everything. Not some abstract, hard-to-fathom kind of love but the day-to-day kind that everyone knows—the kind of love we feel when we look at our spouse and our children, or even our animals. In its purest and most powerful form, this love is not jealous or selfish, but unconditional. This is the reality of realities, the incomprehensibly glorious truth of truths that lives and breathes at the core of everything that exists or that will ever exist.[4]

Dr. Moody, from his studies of NDEs, reported the following:

> Many NDErs enjoy an experience with a personage of light. In most cases, they express that the brilliance of the light is indescribable, yet does not dazzle or hurt the eyes, nor keep them from seeing other obstacles. Almost unanimously, they express that it is a being of light that communicates with them. Some attribute human features to this being, and some do not. In all cases, the NDEr feels an irresistible attraction to this being of light. It is a personal being. It has a very definite personality. The love and warmth which emanate from this being are utterly beyond words, and he feels completely surrounded by it and taken up in it, completely at ease and accepted in the presence of this being.[5]

In another of his books Moody explained, "The person usually meets beings of light. These beings aren't composed of ordinary light. They glow with a beautiful and intense luminescence that seems to permeate everything and fill the person with love. In fact, one person who went through this experience said, 'I could describe this as light or [as] love and it would mean the same thing.' Some say that it's almost like being drenched by a rainstorm of light. They also describe the light as being much brighter than anything we experience on earth. But still, despite its brilliant intensity, it doesn't it doesn't hurt the eyes. Instead, it's warm, vibrant, and alive."[6]

Sometimes the NDEr associates this being with someone they revere in their religion, such as the Savior[7] but most do not. Perhaps it is an ancestor who has reached such a stage of glory. Dr. Moody said, "Some have said that it's neither God nor Jesus, but someone very holy nonetheless."[8]

In fact, Dr. Ritchie, upon visiting the highest realm, stated that "the inhabitants . . . exuded light almost as brilliant as the Christ."[9]

This entity could perhaps be the Holy Ghost, for He is in the world of spirits. If this is so, I suppose that He generally speaks by divine investiture.

Moody further explained:

> It is generally at this point that the NDEr experiences a life review (although it is not universal to all NDErs). As a prelude to the review, the glorious being asks a question such as "What have you done with your life to show me?" or, "What have you done with your life that is sufficient?" . . . Incidentally, all insist that this question, ultimate and profound as it may be in its emotional impact, is not at all asked in condemnation. This being, all seem to agree, does not direct the question to them to accuse or to threaten them, for they still feel the total love

> and acceptance coming from the light, no matter what their answer may be. Rather, the point of the question seems to be to make them think about their lives, to draw them out.[10]

To me, these questions seem a very appropriate way to begin the life review. As one man explained, "I saw everything. I saw my whole life pass right by me. . . . All chronological. All precise. It all just went right by. My whole life"[11]

Let me point out that this life review is not Judgment Day. Scripture clarifies that our judgment day follows our resurrection. However, it seems appropriate to me that, as we transition to the next estate, we review our mortal life, noting what we did well and regretting the times in which our performance is disappointing. I see it as a catalyst, as we begin a new phase of existence, to move forward from our past and improve upon it.

"Come Follow Me"

Our Prophet has given us the charge, and has provided the resources and the process, to strengthen our faith in Heavenly Father and Jesus Christ. It seems appropriate to end this book with four excerpts from glorious near-death experiences to add to our faith in the Father and the Son, illustrate their magnificent glory, and enhance our worship of Them.

> And this enormously bright light seemed almost to cradle me. I just seemed to exist in it and be part of it and be nurtured by it and the feeling just became more and more and more ecstatic and glorious and perfect. And everything about it was—if you took the one thousand best things that ever happened to you in your life and multiplied them by a million, maybe you could get close to this feeling.[12]

> I have never, before or since, seen anything as beautiful, loving and perfectly pleasant as this being. An immense, radiant love poured from it. An incredible light shone through every single pore of its face. The colors of the light were magnificent, vibrant, and alive. The light radiated outward. It was a brilliant white superimposed with what I can only describe as a golden hue. I was filled with an intense feeling of joy and awe.[13]

> I knew that [the light] was omnipotent, that it represented infinite divine love. . . . Even though the light seemed thousands and thousands of times stronger than the brightest sunlight, it did not bother my eyes.[14]

> By my side was a Being with a magnificent presence. I could not see an exact form, but instead, a radiation of light that lit up everything about me and spoke with a voice that held the deepest tenderness one can ever imagine . . . as this loving yet powerful Being spoke to me, I understood vast meanings, much beyond my ability to explain.[15]

In Conclusion

As I stated in the introduction, there is some redundancy in this book. It is in deference to those who choose to read only portions of the book, and to emphasize points that are important to more than one question.

Please know that I do not profess that all the contents of this study are pure truth. Recognizing my imperfect perceptions, I have often included words such as "seemingly," "apparently," and "perhaps." At the same time, I have tried not to overuse such "disclaimers" to avoid them becoming cumbersome.

I can say in total certainty that writing this book has increased my recognition of my weakness in expressing what I wish to convey, while also making a sincere attempt to avoid suggesting that all my observations are accurate.

Perhaps I have felt the same sentiment expressed by the great prophet Moroni: "When [I] write [I] behold [my] weakness, and stumble because of the placing of [my] words; and I fear lest the [readers] will mock at [my] words (Ether 12:25).

I hope that this book may lead you to a better understanding of the first three phases of our eternal life, provide needed comfort, enhance understanding of this laboratory called mortality, lend hope for our next life, and inspire improvement in this one.

NOTES

1. Ring, *Headed Toward Omega*, 53.
2. Ibid., 55.
3. Ibid., 58.
4. Alexander, *Proof of Heaven,* 112.
5. Moody, *Life after Life,* 43.
6. Moody, *The Light Beyond,* 12.
7. Moody, *Life after Life,* 46.
8. Moody, *The Light Beyond,* 13.
9. Ritchie, *Ordered to Return,* 45.
10. Ibid., 45.

11. Ring, 61.
12. Ibid., 62.
13. Ibid., 65.
14. Ibid., 66.
15. Ibid., 75.

WORKS CITED

Alexander, Eben. *Proof of Heaven.* New York: Simon and Schuster, 2012. Written by a neurosurgeon who, prior to his NDE, had lived a very analytical life. He subsequently recognizes the superiority of the spiritual body to the mortal body, particularly the immortal mind to the mortal brain. Though the book is about three-fourths "filler," it includes some well-expressed thoughts relative to the supreme importance of the spiritual aspect of life and love.

Benson, Ezra Taft. "Christ—Gifts and Expectations." *Ensign,* Dec. 1988. See churchofjesuschrist.org/study/ensign/1988/12/jesus-christ-gifts-and-expectations?lang=eng.

———. "To the Children of the Church." *Ensign*, May 1989. See churchofjesuschrist.org/study/ensign/1989/05/to-the-children-of-the-church?lang=eng.

Baxter, David S. "Faith, Fortitude, Fulfillment: A Message to Single Parents." *Ensign,* May 2012. See churchofjesuschrist.org/study/ensign/2012/05/saturday-afternoon-session/faith-fortitude-fulfillment-a-message-to-single-parents?lang=eng.

A Book of Mormon Treasury. Salt Lake City: Deseret Book, 2003.

Borgia, Anthony. *Here and Hereafter.* London: Psychic Press, 1968. Dictated by Robert Hugh Benson in 1957. You must read the entries for *Life in the World Unseen* and *More Life in the World Unseen* to understand this synopsis because it is the third volume dictated by Benson. It was written to answer questions generated by the first two books. It is somewhat redundant of his two other books but adds new and enlightening information.

———. *Life in the World Unseen*. Midway, UT: M.A.P., 1993. This "testimonial" of the spirit world is an enigma! The book is an exploration of the spirit world, but not from an NDE. Rather, it is purportedly dictated to Anthony Borgia by Monsignor Robert Hugh Benson, who is dead. Benson (1871–1914) was the son of Edward White Benson, Archbishop of Canterbury. Robert followed in his father's ecclesiastical footsteps and became an Anglican priest. As he studied and began writing—he authored thirty-six books (thirteen of a religious nature) and several plays—he became uneasy in his own doctrinal position. He converted to Roman Catholicism and became a chamberlain to the pope before dying at age forty-two. In the spirit world, he recognized the error of the theology he had written in mortality and yearned to communicate that truth to the mortal world. Those who presided over him in the spirit world told him that he could not express his message to the mortal world "for some years to come." I don't know precisely when he first communicated his message—his effort to "set things right"—but the book I own was published in 1993 by M.A.P. in Midway, Utah. The company no longer exists, and I can find no record of it. The book does not mention Christ directly but alludes to Him strongly. As I compare Monsignor Benson's description of the spirit world to revealed doctrine, I deem his contribution to be of great value.

———. *More About Life in the World Unseen*. Midway, UT: M.A.P., 2000. Recorded by Anthony Borgia, as dictated by Robert Hugh Benson. Borgia states that this dictation (Benson's second book, after *Life in the World Unseen*) was presented in 1951, thirty-seven years after Benson's death. It is essentially Benson's narrative of the introductory tour of the spirit world for a recently deceased young man. He is assigned to Benson and an associate for spirit world orientation.

Burpo, Todd, with Vincent, Lynn. *Heaven Is for Real*. Nashville: Thomas Nelson, 2010. A cute book (and also a movie) about the NDE of a three-year-old boy, told in the purity and sincerity of a child. His father, a Christian minister, learns simple truths from his son's NDE that are in conflict with his theological training. For example, his son teaches him that the Trinity is composed of three distinct beings. The book contains a lot of filler material, and the spirit world experiences could have been told in about one-third as many pages.

Crowther, Duane S. *Life Everlasting: A Definitive Study of Life After Death*. Bountiful, UT: Horizon, 1967. This book was first published in 1967. More than 150 pages were added thirty years later. Crowther was the "pioneer" member of the Church to write thoroughly researched books concerning the future of this world and our hereafter. *Life Everlasting* addresses not only the spirit world but also man's journey all the way to (we hope) exaltation. The book received immediate widespread readership due to the quality of writing and the many new concepts it introduced, supported by meticulously researched documentation. More than 100,000 copies were in circulation by 1970, when other books began to be published on the subject and received worldwide circulation. Many of them cited it and referred to the experiences Crowther cited. Over the years, sales of *Life Everlasting* have climbed to more than a half million copies, and the book retains its position as one of the most significant books on life after death in print. As one of the most renowned "restored Church of Jesus Christ" authors of all time, Crowther has written fifty-six books, nearly thirty on gospel topics.

Doctrine and Covenants Student Manual. The Church of Jesus Christ of Latter-day Saints, 1981.

Eadie, Betty J. *Embraced by the Light.* New York: Bantam Books, 1992. Number one *New York Times* best seller. Sister Eadie was raised on an Indian reservation. She converted to The Church of Jesus Christ of Latter-day Saints but drifted into inactivity until after her NDE. The book's sales demonstrate its appeal. It is an easy, joyful read centered on divine love. It has inspired multitudes and provided hope to the heavy-hearted.

Encyclopedia of Latter-day Saint History. Edited by Arnold K. Garr, et al. Salt Lake City: Deseret Book, 2000.

Faust, James E. "The Atonement: Our Greatest Hope." *Ensign,* Nov. 2001. See churchofjesuschrist.org/study/ensign/2001/11/the-atonement-our-greatest-hope.html?lang=eng#title1.

———. "Dear Are the Sheep That Have Wandered." *Ensign* May 2003. See churchofjesuschrist.org/study/ensign/2003/05/dear-are-the-sheep-that-have-wandered?lang=eng.

———. "A Royal Priesthood." *Ensign*, May 2006. See churchofjesuschrist.org/study/ensign/2006/05/a-royal-priesthood.html?lang=eng#title1.

———. "The Voice of the Spirit." *Ensign*, Nov. 1994. See churchofjesuschrist.org/study/ensign/1994/04/the-voice-of-the-spirit?lang=eng.

———. "Woman, Why Weepest Thou?" *Ensign*, Nov. 1996. See churchofjesuschrist.org/study/ensign/1996/11/woman-why-weepest-thou?lang=eng.

Hales, Robert D. "The Covenant of Baptism: To Be in the Kingdom and of the Kingdom." *Ensign*, Nov. 2000. See churchofjesuschrist.org/study/ensign/2000/11/the-covenant-of-baptism-to-be-in-the-kingdom-and-of-the-kingdom?lang=eng.

Haraldsson, Erlendur, PhD, and Karlis Osis, PhD. *At the Hour of Death.* Norwalk, CT: Hastings House, 1997.

Hill, Mary V. *Angel Children.* Bountiful, UT: Horizon, 1973. This booklet was given to us by a friend. She had found some comfort from it after losing a child. When we lost our son, she hoped it might also provide some comfort for us. Written by a woman who lost a child, it quotes Church leaders, scriptures, and several prominent Church members. It supports the concept that the death of a child is not haphazard but foreordained.

Hinckley, Gordon B. "Faith in Every Footstep: The Epic Pioneer Journey." *Ensign*, May 1997. See churchofjesuschrist.org/study/ensign/1997/05/faith-in-every-footstep-the-epic-pioneer-journey?lang=eng.

———. "Lessons I Learned as a Boy." *Ensign*, May 1993. See churchofjesuschrist.org/study/ensign/1993/05/some-lessons-i-learned-as-a-boy?lang=eng.

Holland, Jeffrey R. "The Ministry of Angels." *Ensign*, Nov. 2008. See churchofjesuschrist.org/study/ensign/2008/11/the-ministry-of-angels?lang=eng.

Hunter, Howard W. "The Temptations of Christ." *Ensign*, Nov. 1976. See churchofjesuschrist.org/study/ensign/1976/11/the-temptations-of-christ?lang=eng.

Ingersoll, Robert Green. *Greatest Speeches of Col. R. G. Ingersoll.* Chicago: Rhodes and McClure, 1985.

Improvement Era, Oct. 1929.

Journal of Discourses. 26 vols. London: Latter-day Saints' Book Depot, 1854–86.

Kimball, Spencer W. "Tragedy or Destiny?" Salt Lake City: Deseret Book, 1977.

Klebingat, Jorg. "Defending the Faith." *Ensign*, Sept. 2017. See churchofjesuschrist.org/study/ensign/2017/09/defending-the-faith.html.

Lee, Harold B. Area conference, Munich, Germany, 1973.

Lewis, C. S. *Mere Christianity.* San Franciso: Harper-Collins, 1943. The Brethren probably quote this renowned Christian theologian more than any other Christian who is not a member of The Church of Jesus Christ of Latter-day Saints. Lewis was British and taught at both Cambridge and Oxford. Until age thirty-two, he called himself an atheist, but influenced by J.R.R. Tolkien, Rudyard Kipling, and others, he became an ardent advocate of Christianity, in word and in deed. He authored more than thirty books (including *The Chronicles of Narnia*), most of them testifying in powerful prose of Christ and His attributes.

———. *Weight of Glory.* San Francisco: Harper-Collins, 2015.

Maxwell, Neal A. *But for a Small Moment.* Salt Lake City: Deseret Book, 1986. In his typical elegant prose, Elder Maxwell compares the emphasis of Joseph Smith's teachings before his incarceration in Liberty Jail with what he emphasized in the years after his release. Elder Maxwell postulates that the challenges of being the Prophet of the Restoration had kept Joseph Smith so occupied that he had little time to deeply study and ponder his revelations until he was confined for five months. Two chapters are dedicated to the Prophet's post-imprisonment teachings about premortality.

———. "Endure It Well." *Ensign,* May 1990. See churchofjesuschrist.org/study/ensign/1990/05/endure-it-well?lang=eng.

———. "How Choice a Seer!" *Ensign,* Nov. 2003. See churchofjesuschrist.org/study/ensign/2003/11/how-choice-a-seer.html?lang=eng#title1.

———. "Premortality, a Glorious Reality." *Ensign*, Nov. 1985. See churchofjesuschrist.org/study/ensign/1985/11/premortality-a-glorious-reality?lang=eng.

———. *The Promise of Discipleship.* Salt Lake City: Deseret Book, 2001. Elder Maxwell wrote more than thirty books. This one includes a chapter about the spirit world and was written just three years before the author's death.

———. "The Women of God." *Ensign*, May 1978. See churchofjesuschrist.org/study/ensign/1978/05/the-women-of-god?lang=eng.

McConkie, Bruce R. "The Dead Who Die in the Lord." *Ensign*, Nov. 1976. See churchofjesuschrist.org/study/ensign/1976/11/the-dead-who-die-in-the-lord?lang=eng.

———. "God Foreordains His Prophets and People." *Ensign*, May 1974. See churchofjesuschrist.org/study/ensign/1974/05/god-foreordains-his-prophets-and-his-people?lang=eng.

———. *Mormon Doctrine*. Salt Lake City: Bookcraft, 1987.

Menet, Sarah LaNell. *There Is No Death*. Phillipsburg, MT: Mountain Top, 2002. Menet's book contains a lot of filler leading up to her NDE; however, her descriptions in the NDE substantiate many of the principles presented in *Where Do We Go From Here*. Her NDE includes a look into the future that parallels portions of Cedar Fort's book *Visions of Glory*.

Moody, Raymond. *The Light Beyond*. New York: Bantam Books, 1988. Moody has not personally experienced an NDE, but he has made a study of the experiences of others and has written several books. This one offers synopses of the work of several researchers. He feels that NDEs have two irrefutable proofs: (1) everyone he knows of who has experienced an NDE (including those researched by others) has returned happier and more dedicated to higher purposes than before, and (2) many who have experienced an NDE can give precise detail of the events in the hospital (even some that occurred in a different area in the hospital) while the person was "dead." For example, Moody cites the experience of a woman, blind from age eighteen, who experienced an NDE at age seventy. She could precisely describe events, persons, and even medical instruments utilized while she was "dead."

———. *Life after Life*. Covington, GA: Mockingbird Books, 1975. (One of three books by Dr. Moody in this bibliography.) In this early scientific study of NDEs, Moody explores experiences that are common to many who have experienced an NDE, and he explains why they could not be conjured up by the throes of a dying brain. He expresses some of the weakness of science that inhibits its recognition of NDEs. Although Dr. Moody does not share his religious views, he refers favorably to "Mormons" (his word) several times in his three books.

———. *Reflections on Life After Life*. Covington, GA: Mockingbird Books, 1978. Dr. Moody adds insights derived from additional research since writing *Life After Life*. Of interest to members of the Church, he says: "It is noteworthy that members of The Church of Jesus Christ of Latter-day Saints (the Mormons) have been aware of accounts of near-death experiences for many years and circulate these stories among themselves." He perhaps does not realize that this is just the tip of the iceberg: the Church is certainly doing work in behalf of the dead that is unprecedented in any religion, Christian or otherwise.

Neal, Mary C. *To Heaven and Back.* Colorado Springs, CO: WaterBrook Press, 2013. Number one *New York Times* best seller. The Christian author is an orthopedic surgeon, which perhaps adds credibility to her NDE. While it adds but little new information about the spirit world, it is a powerful testate of the love of God.

Nelson, Lee. *Beyond the Veil,* vol. 1. Springville, UT: Cedar Fort, 1988. Lee Nelson is a popular LDS author. This volume is a compilation of near-death experiences (NDEs), primarily from Latter-day Saints. There is little commentary.

Nelson, Russell M., and Wendy Watson Nelson. "Hope of Israel." Worldwide Youth Devotional, June 3, 2018.

Oaks, Dallin H. "The Aaronic Priesthood and the Sacrament." *Ensign*, Nov. 1998. See churchofjesuschrist.org/study/ensign/1998/11/the-aaronic-priesthood-and-the-sacrament?lang=eng.

———. "Apostasy and Restoration." *Ensign*, May 1995. See churchofjesuschrist.org/study/ensign/1995/05/apostasy-and-restoration?lang=eng.

———. "The Great Plan of Happiness." *Ensign*, Nov. 1993. See churchofjesuschrist.org/study/ensign/1993/11/the-great-plan-of-happiness?lang=eng.

———. "Trust in the Lord." *Ensign*, Nov. 2019. See churchofjesuschrist.org/study/ensign/2019/11/17oaks?lang=eng.

Packer, Boyd K. "The Gift of the Holy Ghost." *Ensign*, Nov. 1994. See churchofjesuschrist.org/study/friend/1995/07/the-gift-of-the-holy-ghost?lang=eng.

Rampton, Ryan. J. *You Were Born a Warrior: A Near Death Experience.* Independently published, 2018.

Ring, Kenneth, PhD. *Heading Toward Omega.* New York: Quill, 1984. Like Dr. Moody's books, this book is a scientific study of NDEs, garnered from 111 peoples' experiences. Ring focuses much of his book on how an NDE affects a person.

Ritchie, George G. Jr. *Ordered to Return*. Charlottesville, VA: Hampton Roads, 1998. The follow-up book to *Return from Tomorrow*, this book is a magnificent example of how an NDE can enhance one's life. Dr. Ritchie believes that his orientation to the spirit world was hosted by the Savior. Dr. Ritchie thereafter dedicated his life to advocating Christ and exhorting others to follow His example. As a follower of Christ, he has tried to especially serve the downtrodden. Although not a member of the Church, Ritchie mentions it twice. First, he uses some of the Church's three degrees of glory nomenclature in describing the realms of the spirit world. Second, he states, "We all need to be ashamed of the way we treated our Mormon brothers and sisters when they began."

———. *Return from Tomorrow*. Grand Rapids, MI: Baker Book House, 1978. This book essentially "opened the door" for lending credence to NDEs and it has been immensely popular. My copy, printed in 2004, was from the thirty-third printing. Ritchie's obvious character and multiple advanced degrees (including a doctorate in psychiatry) lend him great respect and credibility. A friend gave this book to me when our son was killed, and I subsequently passed it on to a friend who lost his wife in a traffic accident. It provided both comfort and insight, and I suppose that pattern has happened thousands of times. Dr. Ritchie is not a member of the Church, but he speaks positively of it (see *Ordered to Return*).

Rotstein, Gary. "Near Death, Seeing Dead People May be Neither Rare nor Eerie." *Standard Examiner*, July 10, 2018.

Scott, Richard G. "How to Obtain Revelation and Inspiration for Your Personal Life." *Ensign*, May 2012. See churchofjesuschrist.org/study/ensign/2012/05/saturday-afternoon-session/how-to-obtain-revelation-and-inspiration-for-your-personal-life?lang=eng.

Smith, Joseph Fielding. "The Sin against the Holy Ghost." *Instructor*, Oct. 1935. See also *Doctrines of Salvation*, 1:47–48.

Smith, Lucy Mack. *The Revised and Enhanced History of Joseph Smith by His Mother*. Salt Lake City: Book Craft, 1996.

Springer, Rebecca Ruter. *My Dream of Heaven*. LaVerne, TN: White Crow Books, 2009. Although this book was recently published, the experience related took place not long after the American Civil War (1861–65). I include this book because the author, not a member of the Church, references eternal marriage.

Swedenborg, Emanuel. *Heaven and Hell.* 1758. Quotes from this book are taken from Brent and Wendy Top's publication *Glimpses Beyond Death's Door,* which is included in this section. Swedenborg was a renowned Swedish theologian, scientist, and mystic. He claimed numerous revelations concerning the afterlife. Some fit so well with Church doctrine that some enemies of the Church claim that Joseph Smith plagiarized Swedenborg, just as some of them have pushed the now widely discredited theory that the Book of Mormon was plagiarized from a Spaulding manuscript.

Smith, Joseph. *Teachings of the Prophet Joseph Smith.* Selected by Joseph Fielding Smith. Salt Lake City: Deseret Book, 1976. Joseph Fielding Smith compiled this book while he was serving both as an Apostle and as Church Historian in 1938. It is my favorite book of all gospel literature.

Smith, Joseph F. *Gospel Doctrine.* Salt Lake City: Deseret Book, 1919.

Teachings of Presidents of the Church—Brigham Young. Salt Lake City: The Church of Jesus Christ of Latter-day Saints, 1997. A magnificent resource, published by the Church, as a manual for the Melchizedek Priesthood and the Relief Society. Chapters 37 and 38 give great insight into the spirit world. This manual has great credibility because it comes from a prophet, and it has also been through Church correlation. President Young had apparently experienced the difficulty of returning to our fallen world after experiencing a visit to the spirit paradise because he states, "I have had to exercise a great deal more faith to desire to live than I ever exercised in my whole life to live."

Teachings of Presidents of the Church—Harold B. Lee. Salt Lake City: The Church of Jesus Christ of Latter-day Saints, 2000.

Teachings of Presidents of the Church—Joseph Smith. Salt Lake City: The Church of Jesus Christ of Latter-day Saints, 2007.

Top, Brent L., and Wendy C. *Glimpses Beyond Death's Door.* American Fork, UT: Covenant Communications, 2012. Brother Top has served in significant positions in the Church Educational System and as a stake president and mission president. The book provides insights from Church leaders and from persons who have experienced NDEs.

Young, Brigham. *Discourses of Brigham Young.* Compiled by John A. Widtsoe. Salt Lake City: Deseret Book, 1954.

ABOUT THE AUTHOR

Wesley White proudly wore the uniform of the United States Air Force for thirty-six years: as an ROTC cadet at BYU, a command pilot, and an Air Force JrROTC instructor. He accrued 5,000 military flying hours (including the testing of "stealth" technology) and directed the Air Force's interaction with Latin America's air forces. He retired at the rank of Lieutenant Colonel.

He served seven years as a full-time missionary (as a young man in the Spanish-American Mission, as president of the Florida Orlando Mission, and as director of the Mesa Arizona Temple Visitors' Center) plus eight years as a stake president. He currently serves as a sealer in the Ogden Utah Temple.

Wesley earned a BA in communicative arts from Brigham Young University and a master of public administration graduate degree from the University of Oklahoma. He is the father of six living children.